9/03

Contents

THE RISE OF
WOMEN ENTREPRENEURS

People, Processes, and Global Trends

Jeanne Halladay Coughlin
with
Andrew R. Thomas

QUORUM BOOKS
Westport, Connecticut • London

Library of Congress Cataloging-in-Publication Data

Coughlin, Jeanne Halladay, 1963–
  The rise of women entrepreneurs : people, processes, and global trends /
Jeanne Halladay Coughlin with Andrew R. Thomas.
    p. cm.
  Includes bibliographical references and index.
  ISBN 1–56720–462–7 (alk. paper)
  1. Self-employed women. 2. Businesswomen. 3. Women-owned business
enterprises. 4. Entrepreneurship—Case studies. 5. Self-employed women—
Developing countries. 6. Businesswomen—Developing countries. 7. Women-
owned business enterprises—Developing countries. 8. Entrepreneurship—
Developing countries—Case studies. I. Thomas, Andrew R. II. Title.
  HD6072.5 .C68 2002
  338'.04'082091724—dc21   2001058935

British Library Cataloguing in Publication Data is available.

Library of Congress Catalog Card Number: 2001058935
ISBN: 1–56720–462–7

First published in 2002

Quorum Books, 88 Post Road West, Westport, CT 06881
An imprint of Greenwood Publishing Group, Inc.
www.quorumbooks.com

Printed in the United States of America

The paper used in this book complies with the
Permanent Paper Standard issued by the National
Information Standards Organization (Z39.48–1984).

10 9 8 7 6 5 4 3 2

Illustrations

Acknowledgments

Being a female entrepreneur is one of the most rewarding roles I have undertaken in life. I feel fortunate to have the opportunity to explore, examine, and celebrate the topic of female entrepreneurship in this book.

I would like to recognize and thank Wendy Keller from Forthwrite Literary Agency for believing in this book and for her success as a woman business owner.

Thank you also to Eric Valentine from Quorum Publishing for your confidence in me, your vision for the book, and your guidance in helping to create a quality product.

This book could not have been written without the intellect, research skills, and writing talent of Andrew R. Thomas. I feel fortunate to have you as a coauthor and friend.

Thank you to my parents, Jeanne and Kenneth Halladay, who raised a family of seven children, including two female entrepreneurs! You gave me the greatest gift a child can have—a close, loving family.

Even more rewarding than the role I play as a female entrepreneur are the roles I play as wife and mother. Thank you to my best friend and biggest supporter, Kevin—you have stuck with me through it all.

I dedicate this book to my daughters, Katherine and Emma. Having you was a success beyond any I can ever achieve in business. I hope that my desire to achieve my dreams will inspire you to pursue yours.

Introduction

Across the globe, women are starting businesses in record numbers. In the United States, for example, women own 9.1 million firms, or 38 percent of all U.S. companies. From 1987 to 1999, the number of woman-owned firms in the United States increased by 103 percent; employment by female companies rose 320 percent; and, even more astounding, sales grew by 436 percent. Female-owned businesses in the United States generate more than $3.6 trillion in annual sales, and female entrepreneurs employ more people than the entire Fortune 500.

Although the United States may be the most reported example of the rise of female entrepreneurs within the industrialized world, woman-owned businesses are on the rise everywhere. In eastern Germany, women have created a third of the new enterprises since reunification in 1990, providing 1 million new jobs and contributing U.S. $15 billion to the German gross national product. Female entrepreneurs in other transition economies, like Russia, Hungary, Romania, and Poland, are making a similar impact. In Latin America, according to the World Bank, fully half of all economic growth in the last decade throughout the region is attributable to the creativity and hard work of female entrepreneurs. In South Asia, women now outnumber men as business owners. And in Southeast Asia female-owned businesses have been at the forefront of that region's economic turnaround since the "Asian flu" arrived in 1997.

Clearly, the growth of female enterprises is good for economies. What may be less evident, though, is that the rise of female entrepreneurs also benefits societies and women themselves. Those who desire to see the conditions for women improve all over the world have discovered the incomparable value of nurturing and cultivating female entrepreneurship. The benefits derived when women start and operate their own businesses are truly remarkable: increased self-esteem, quality of life, and life expectancy as well as reduced infant mortality, incidences of AIDS and other diseases, and domestic violence.

This book provides an examination of the fundamental issues facing female entrepreneurship from a global perspective. Divided into three separate sections, the book looks at the major areas of study concerning women business owners today: the global trend of female entrepreneurship; the characteristics and motivations of the women who start their own enterprises; and the processes women undertake to start their own businesses. The book concludes with ways that organizations—private, public, and governmental—can effectively support female entrepreneurship and continuously monitor and evaluate their efforts.

In Part I, "The Trend," we seek to provide the reader with the global perspective to recognize the unstoppable rising tide of female entrepreneurship around the world. Chapter 1, "The Rise of Female Entrepreneurs," addresses the exponential growth in woman-owned businesses in developed and developing countries. Underscored is the fact that the tremendous rise of female entrepreneurship is one of the most significant economic and social developments in the world.

In the developing world, woman-owned "micro-enterprises" have begun to attract much attention as well. Charitable and nonprofit organizations working at the grassroots have found that investing in female entrepreneurs offers the most effective means to improve health, nutrition, hygiene, and educational standards for women and their children.

Chapter 2, "Women and Globalization," explores the impact of the expansion of the global economy on women. It goes without saying that globalization is probably shaping the future of all human beings more than any other single force at work in the world today. For this reason, the chapter undertakes an analysis of globalization as it relates to the hopes and dreams of female entrepreneurs.

Chapter 3, "The Empowerment of Women," investigates the definition of this much-used term within the context of woman-owned businesses.

Part II, "The Participants," focuses on female enterprises by looking at the characteristics of the women who start them and addressing their primary motivations.

Chapter 4, "Women As Business Owners," looks at how fostering the participation of women entrepreneurs strengthens economies and can be a source of political, economic, and social innovation. Women business owners, in comparison with their male counterparts, often have different demands on their time and different ways of seeing things and may be newer to the market. They therefore do business differently from men and, consequently, constitute a real potential source of innovation in management style, company structure, services rendered to the community, and the use of technology, among other things.

Clearly, no single factor inspires a woman to build her own company. Her reasons depend on several personal and external circumstances, both positive and negative. Chapters 5, 6, and 7 explore women's primary and most deep-seated motivations for starting and running their own businesses: economic, social, and personal.

In Part III, "The Processes," we begin with the premise that women often establish businesses for different reasons than men do. And they typically start businesses in different markets and with different business structures.

Chapter 8, "Challenges Faced by Female Entrepreneurs," explores the fundamental distinctions between female entrepreneurs and their male counterparts and delves into several issues that are unique to female startups.

Chapter 9, "Tools and Processes for Helping Female Entrepreneurs," furnishes evaluative tools for a woman seeking to start her own business. Such an assessment enables the prospective woman business owner to better discern the sources of assistance at her disposal.

Chapter 10, "Locating and Evaluating Potential Help Givers," prepares the potential female entrepreneur to determine which help givers to engage and how to best approach them.

Chapter 11 looks at female entrepreneuership from the perspective of those organizations dedicated to supporting female-owned enterprises. Further, it details a scheme to provide donors, project managers, and policy analysts with the tools needed for assessing the available entry strategies and metrics for conducting ongoing analysis of project effectiveness. It is a road map for those entities looking to maximize the effectiveness of their programs and projects. As a result, they can put into place effective monitoring and evaluation metrics.

The appendixes furnish the reader with the most comprehensive global resource guide for anyone interested in learning more about female entrepreneurs and woman-owned businesses.

We admit wholeheartedly that each of these topics could themselves warrant its own book or even series of books. Moreover, we recognize that some important issues may be too lightly touched on or not discussed at all. Our intent here is simply to inspire constructive dialogue and energetic action on female entrepreneurship around the world.

If anything is clear, it is that the number of female-owned businesses will do nothing but increase worldwide in the coming years. Therefore, it is incumbent upon everyone involved with female entrepreneurs to better understand the trend, the participants, the processes, and the helpers in this most important phenomenon. As Lucite Moot said some 150 years ago:

Let women then go on—not asking favors, but claiming as a right the removal of all hindrances to her elevation in the scale of being—let her receive the encouragement for the proper cultivation of all her powers, so that she may enter profitably into the active business of life.

PART I

THE TREND

1

The Rise of Women Entrepreneurs

Why is it we rarely hear of a self-made woman?
                                        Anonymous query

Women everywhere are becoming entrepreneurs. In greater numbers than ever before, women are stepping away from traditional economic roles and venturing out to start to their own businesses. In every field imaginable, even the most "masculine," you don't have to look hard to find female entrepreneurs who have overcome seemingly impossible odds to achieve success.

The profound structural changes taking place in the nations of the world are providing new opportunities for entrepreneurs—male and female alike. In the industrialized countries, manufacturing is in decline, but the rapidly growing service industries are burgeoning. In this rapid change and ensuing disarray brought about by the globalization of markets and competition, new technology, and instantaneous communications, the old way of doing things is proving ineffective and obsolete. New opportunities abound—and women are taking advantage of them.[1]

In many developing countries, manufacturing is on the rise and modernization is coming very quickly. As in industrialized nations, change is occurring at an accelerated pace. During this period of fluidity and flux, ambitious, energetic, and creative individuals are seizing the initiative. As a result, women are also becoming a driving force in the growth of emerging and developing economies around the world.

Needless to say, the significant changes in the world economy have greatly altered the status of women in the marketplace. New opportunities have generated new challenges—meeting the greater demand for skills and specialization of knowledge, maintaining the viability of those skills and that knowledge in an ever-changing marketplace, and accommodating the instability that can arise from such changes. As a result, new ways of thinking and doing have to be considered. At such a juncture, the leadership style of women and their special capacities and qualities appear especially valuable.

In addition to structural transformation, changes in values also are taking place. Changing social forces encourage women to enter the realm of the workplace and business ownership. Since World War II, there has been a growing influx of women into western labor markets, motivated in part by the need they feel for financial independence and self-sufficiency. Other factors include the inadequacy of one paycheck today to meet the financial needs of many middle-class families, a growing divorce rate, and an increasing number of women as heads of households. Moreover, changing values and attitudes toward paid work also encourage some financially secure women to seek self-realization outside the home.[2]

This emerging pattern in the developed world has found an echo in the developing world. In country after country, development agencies have discovered the importance of women's contributions to the local economy and their potential as key contributors in promoting sustainable development at the grassroots.

Whether in the west or in the developing world, however, not all women are content to be employees. A growing number are emerging as entrepreneurs.

According to a series of studies conducted and analyzed by the National Foundation for Women Business Owners (NFWBO):

• Across the world, woman-owned firms typically constitute between one-fourth and one-third of the business population
• The number of woman-owned enterprises is growing faster than the economy at large in many countries
• Woman-owned businesses are starting in every industrial sector

"Entrepreneurship among women is a vibrant and growing trend internationally," noted NFWBO director of research Julie R. Weeks. "Women business owners are making significant contributions to economic health and competitiveness in countries around the world."

These are women who choose, for their own account, to organize and manage the resources of their own companies and assume the financial risks inherent in doing so in the hope of eventually earning a profit. For low-income women, the primary motivation is to generate income. At the same time, for many women entrepreneurs, objectives like self-fulfillment or fostering a worthwhile cause are as important as profits. At one extreme, their enterprises may be as small as their own part-time work. At another, they may grow into such large enterprises as The Body Shop, an international chain of natural cosmetics founded by Anita Roddick with annual sales in excess of $1.2 billion.[3]

WOMEN ENTREPRENEURS IN THE INDUSTRIALIZED WORLD

Female entrepreneurs play a vital role in creating wealth and jobs. In the face of global competition, large manufacturers in the industrialized world are constantly "downsizing" by reorganizing and laying off workers. The resulting uncertainties are of great political, social, and economic concern. In this unstable economic environment, entrepreneurial firms are creators of jobs. Firms with fewer than twenty employees provide a quarter of all jobs. A growing number of these small, new companies are led by women.

In the United States companies owned by women provide 12 million jobs, while the 500 largest firms, the Fortune 500, employ slightly fewer: 11.7 million jobs. Furthermore, these Fortune 500 companies are shedding 200,000 to 300,000 employees each year.[4]

Female entrepreneurs are innovators, and innovation stimulates general economic growth. Towns that once depended on a single large manufacturer now recognize the wisdom of attracting small entrepreneurial companies. The resulting diversification contributes to the stability and resiliency of the local economy. Greater local ownership also adds stability, since people who live and work in a community and who serve their neighbors have a personal stake in its well-being. In addition, entrepreneurship is a means of providing economic opportunity for disadvantaged groups, including women, low-wage earners, and minorities.

Women entrepreneurs make another important contribution to economic development by creating wealth as well as jobs. From 1980 to 1988 the number of entrepreneurs in the United States increased 56 percent while the number of female entrepreneurs among these increased 82 percent. Over the same period, the rate of growth in revenue of women's enterprises more than doubled that of the entrepreneurial sector as a whole.

In the world's wealthiest countries, there is great diversity of characteristics shared by women who are entrepreneurs or who aspire to create their own economic activity. Some already are professionals or well-educated people with corporate managerial experience. Others have gained experience through the unpaid work of home management and motherhood. Still others live in a fourth world as the urban poor in wealthy nations and may have little schooling or work experience

The rise of women entrepreneurs in industrialized countries is recent. Before 1970 women entrepreneurs were rare. Since then, however, their increase has been remarkable. An article published by the Paris-based Organization for Economic Cooperation and Development (OECD)[5] calls it "one of the most significant economic and social developments in the world."[6]

New enterprise creation in the industrialized world by men and women differ from country to country. In the United States women create new enterprises half again as frequently as do men. Nationwide, women own 9.1 million businesses, or 38 percent of all U.S. companies. Female-owned businesses in the United States generate more than $3.6 trillion in annual sales. From 1987 to 1999, the number of woman-owned firms in the United States increased by 103 percent, employment by 320 percent, and sales by 436 percent. Women entrepreneurs in the United States employ 27.5 million people.

Even more encouraging, firms owned by minority women are increasing at triple the national rate. Data from 1996 indicated that one in eight (13 percent) of the woman-owned businesses in the United States was owned by a woman of color.[7]

In Canada, women own about 22 percent of all companies with paid employees. Women represent the fastest-growing segment of the small business sector. Between 1980 and 1985 they were responsible for more than half the increase in owner-operated businesses.

Women entrepreneurs in Canada have staying power. A recent study found that 47 percent of woman-owned businesses were still in business after five years, as compared with 25 percent for men. Nevertheless, women appear to have more difficulty than men in obtaining startup capital, even though their default rate in at least one business loan program (the Ontario New Ventures Program) is about half the rate for male entrepreneurs. A study by the Canadian Federation of Independent Business found that collateral requirements for women were higher than for comparable male entrepreneurs. Other studies have reported similar findings.[8]

Since 1990, women in eastern Germany have created a third of the new enterprises, providing 1 million new jobs and contributing $15 billion annually to the gross national product.

Viola Winkler[9]

Viola Winkler is a woman on the go. When not dashing to catch a flight to one of her branch offices in Hamburg, Frankfurt, or Moscow, she often spends late nights organizing trade fairs on starting small businesses.

Ms. Winkler is head of the Saxony Training Institute in Dresden, Germany, which trains prospective entrepreneurs in management, marketing, and other business skills. When an important call comes in, she springs from the meeting table and darts for her office, her heels leaving indentations in the blue-carpeted hallway.

A lot of other eastern German women would like to follow in her tracks. One-third of eastern German businesses are owned by women, compared with one-fourth to one-fifth in western Germany, according to the German Federal Labor Bureau. Women head 150,000 firms employing roughly 1 million people, at a time when German unemployment stands at near-record levels.

One reason many east German women became entrepreneurs is that they were laid off after German unification in 1990. "Women were the first to be removed from the work force," Winkler says. As waves of unprofitable, uncompetitive Communist-era factories were shut down between 1990 and 1995, 1.6 million women lost their jobs, compared with 1.2 million men.

Under Communist rule, more than 90 percent of women worked. The regime, at least officially, sought high female employment on ideological grounds. Some analysts say, however, that the motive was less equality than making sure that families were forced to rely on the state to care for their children. Either way, most east German women today prefer not to stay home. Three times as many east German women as west German women seek to return to jobs after two years of maternity leave—a year less than what they are legally entitled to. "It's a society thing," says Ilona Weisbach, who owns and manages a small textile factory in the town of Hormersdorf, west of Dresden. "We received good training. We worked, and we were used to earning our own living and being independent."

Since Ms. Weisbach opened her factory, it has grown from six to thirty employees, twenty-seven of them women. Weisbach sees her factory as more than just a way of attaining independence and turning a profit. "It's a matter of social responsibility to the people in the region," she says.

Social concerns are a pressing issue for women in Germany. Many see themselves as underrepresented not only in business, but in politics as well. Women have been raising their voices during "Frauen Power Woche," a week of demonstrations, debates, and self-help seminars that kicked off on International Women's Day.

An important source of support, say Weisbach and other businesswomen, is their families. Weisbach's husband, Lothar, in addition to pitching in on domestic chores, is also one of her three male employees. He does everything from maintaining machinery to marketing. But, she makes clear, "I am the boss."

Entrepreneur Winkler, despite her own success, says the situation is indeed difficult for eastern German women. She says they face discrimination not only because of their gender, but also because of western German stereotypes of easterners as unsophisticated and undereducated. "I have two problems [to overcome]," she says, "I'm a woman, and I'm from the east."[10]

Miso Makers in Japan

In many parts of the Kanto region in Japan, the processing of *miso*—an ancient type of soybean—by farming women, etc., has seen resurgence in recent years. A demand for new crops combined with the number of women aiming to become entrepreneurs has helped to reintroduce this traditional Japanese staple to whole new generations of consumers. In Tochigi Prefecture, where *miso* processing is especially common, about sixty groups of women are actively involved in *miso* processing. For example, the Myojin Union of Agricultural Product Processing in Imaichi City produces ten tons of *miso* a year, an incredibly large amount for the labor-intensive product, which sells well in large department stores at about 600 yen (U.S. $4.00) for 500 grams (8 oz.).

WOMEN ENTREPRENEURS IN THE DEVELOPING WORLD

Throughout the world, woman-owned firms typically constitute between one-fourth and one-third of the business population. While women entrepreneurs in both developing countries and developed countries share many characteristics, many more women in the developing world remain illiterate—although not lacking in intelligence, experience, and wisdom—and live in poor rural communities.

Nonetheless, women have always actively participated in their local economies. In Africa, for example, women produce 80 percent of the food. In Asia, they produce 60 percent and in Latin America 40 percent. In many cases, women not only produce food but market it as well, giving them a well-developed knowledge of local markets and customers.

In the Maghreb, embracing Morocco, Algeria, and Tunisia, Muslim women create one in every ten new enterprises. According to Moncef Bouchrara, president of the consulting firm Afkar/Ich'Har, many researchers have failed to notice the emergence of an entrepreneurial class of women in the Arab world: "It is assumed to be non-existent. Nevertheless, it is becoming a clear and observable reality throughout the Mediterranean Basin, including the Maghreb." Also, says Bouchrara, the role of women entrepreneurs hasn't been described correctly: its effects on the modernization of the society have not been properly understood. "Societies throughout the Mediterranean Basin are regarded as patriarchal affairs in which the status of women is greatly inferior to that of men." But thanks to enterprising women that is no longer true. "It has to be admitted that a feminism is developing widely along the southern shores of the Mediterranean, a feminism that is integrated into the basic anthropological values that give society its coherence and internal dynamism." Although in the Maghreb enterprise creation rarely takes the form of legal companies, Bouchrara's research shows that in the informal sector more and more new firms are being started, and many of them are started by women.[11]

In Tunisia, more than 11 percent of the firms launched in the last twenty years were created by women. If one observes that in 1970 only 1 percent of new firms were created by women, one can appreciate the scale of the change that has occurred. In this evolution, social practices have altered before any innovation has occurred in institutions. This has created a demand for modernization in institutions: "Women entrepreneurs are not only the internal product of the cultural dynamic of their societies as they undergo modernization, but also appear as independent actors contributing fully to that modernization," says Bouchrara.

The majority of the impoverished in the world are women and children. The tiny enterprises undertaken by some of these women enable them to improve the quality of life for themselves and their families. These micro-enterprises have begun to attract much attention. Charitable and nonprofit organizations working at the grassroots have found that investing in women offers the most effective means to improve health, nutrition, hygiene, and educational standards. The Foundation for International Community Assistance (FINCA) describes women as the "most dependable, productive, and creative members of impoverished societies."[12]

As women in developing countries acquire competence and experience, and as the artificial barriers to their full participation in the economic life of their communities gradually fall, the integration of feminine values into the workplace should create a more humane and balanced work environment. Because of their unique leadership style, women-run enterprises generally provide a caring, cooperative work environment in which individual growth and development are fostered. At the same time, women's ways of leading are proving themselves particularly effective in today's turbulent economic world.

Another observation worthy of reflection is the convergence of a new paradigm of management and a style of leadership typical of women throughout the world. Globalization of markets and competition, new technology, and instantaneous communication bring with them unprecedented change. This is forcing traditional companies to "reinvent" themselves, to adopt a new model of management that shares some of its features with the leadership traits of women entrepreneurs

The example of the accomplishment of women entrepreneurs may well give credence to the prediction made at the beginning of this century that the "new age will be an age less masculine and more permeated with feminine ideals, or, to speak more exactly, will be an age in which the masculine and feminine elements of civilization will be more evenly balanced."[13]

El Hachmia[14]

Leaving the countryside and going into town to make a fortune by starting one's own firm—that wouldn't be news if the main actor were not a woman, and a woman living in Morocco. Her name is El Hachmia, and she is one of the most striking examples of the new breed of women entrepreneurs. As owner of one of the largest fast-moving consumer goods companies in the Arab world, El Hachmia is becoming a legend, a sort of prophet with more and more followers.

El Hachmia started her firm by reselling imported goods, which she purchased from large distributors, in marginal areas of some of the largest cities in Morocco. El Hachmia saw these markets, which were traditionally underserved by larger companies, who preferred to focus on middle- and upper-class markets, as a tremendous oppportunity. By opening retail stores and introducing new products and services to working-class and lower-middle-class consumers, she was able to secure the business of these customers for the long term as they moved their way up the economic ladder.

A self-made woman who overcame crushing poverty and a male-dominated culture to build her thriving business, she has led the way and inspired countless other women to strike out on their own and start companies.

FEMALE ENTREPRENEURS RESPOND TO ECONOMIC CHANGES

With capital, labor, and goods moving much more rapidly across national boundaries, with the speed of technological change revolutionizing production and information systems, women around the world are operating as economic actors in a distinctly changed environment.

To repeat, in most developed countries, traditional manufacturing is making way for new industries and new services. At the same time, the social and environmental implications of industrial development are convincing most people to reject the notion of "growth at any price." The most dynamic actors are no longer the large corporations, but the small or medium-sized firms that can satisfy the needs arising from the new information technologies and that can be profitable while improving the quality of life. Traditional sources of recruitment will be unable to perform as they used to. Jobs lost during downturns will not simply reappear with the next recovery. Many women will no longer accept traditional low-paying jobs that offer little responsibility and no room for promotion. Economic growth will go together with changes in lifestyles. Innovative firms must be created and innovative entrepreneurs must emerge.

There are encouraging signs that change is happening. New participants are gaining ground in the market, starting new firms, proposing new products and services, and sometimes changing the entrepreneurial culture. A particularly innovative impulse is coming from women. In the past, industrialization has brought more women into the job market, but in the present economic environment a new role for women is emerging.

Up to thirty years ago women entrepreneurs were the exception. They are now an important phenomenon, both socially and economically. Across the world, women are now starting companies at 1.5 times the rate that men are. Since 1972, we have gone from essentially 0 percent of the workforce employed by women in 1972 to about 10 percent to 12 percent of the total global workforce today.[15] Energy is coming from women and not from men.

The gap between female and male entrepreneurship is rapidly being bridged. In 1992 women created 10 percent of the new firms in North Africa, 33 percent in North America (in 1998, 75 percent in the United States), and 40 percent in eastern Germany. Women account for a substantial portion of nonagricultural self-employment: 17 percent in Greece; 22–25 percent in Germany, Italy, and the United Kingdom; 34–39 percent in Japan and Canada; and nearly 50 percent in the United States. In Spain 16 percent of entrepreneurs are women, as against 1984 when they constituted only 9.7 percent.[16]

The phenomenon is important not only from the quantitative point of view. It seems clear that having been excluded from leading firms for a long time, women seem to conceive opportunities in an innovative manner, which could prove to be particularly promising in the new economic environment, especially in all fields where business concerns itself with matters like the quality of life.

THE INFLUENCE OF FEMALE ENTREPRENEURS ON BUSINESS

There is a new vision of enterprise that can be found in women's culture. "Women's household duties," says Elisabeth Fenez, French expert for the European Commission for Economic Studies (ECES), "including child-rearing and the financial practical side of housekeeping, have taught them to use their initiative under what are often difficult circumstances, in other words, to be enterprising and innovative."[17] The history of women's social role has always been full of constraints, but it could now be translated into opportunities—which is precisely what many women are doing.

The ECES and OECD studied women's approach to enterprise creation by looking at the experiences of women who have started new firms with the help of various government–private partnership programs that were designed to stimulate new business opportunities for women. Whether the study takes place in the developed world or in India, Brazil, or China, the same questions always seem to come forward: What drives women to become entrepreneurs? Where do they find energy? How does their idea emerge and how do they go about implementing it?

Almost universally, the women surveyed mention the need to play an active role, to participate, which is to say exist in their own right, and to achieve recognition. They want to gain more independence. Besides its economic and income-generating role, business ownership contributes to a person's equilibrium and sense of fulfillment. This motivation is a powerful one, releasing as it does energy, inventiveness, and will to succeed.

Personal circumstances are often the driving force behind a business. These circumstances are invariably employment-related. Women need money but they cannot find paid work, so after a long period of unsuccessful job hunting, they decide to create their own firms. But when they think about what their firms could do, they also show their own special vision of business.

Christina Vasconcelos[18]

Christina Vasconcelos, 37, is one such woman. Living in Lisbon, Portugal, she felt that children in her city were growing up trapped in an exclusively urban environment. That's why she and a friend, unbeknownst to their husbands, borrowed 5,000 cruzeros (about U.S. $5,000) against their credit cards to set up "Terra-a-Terra" ("Land to Land"), a firm providing countryside holidays for children so that they could become more familiar with the rural environment and its lifestyle. She notes: "Innovation is born out of necessity. When an idea meets a large-scale demand, innovation can become a profitable business opportunity."

In other cases, the driving force is not job hunting, but some form of discontent with the situation at the workplace: examples can be low pay or the lack of career prospects in firms that prefer to promote men. That is the story of Fotini Papadopoulou and Penelope Konstandoudi.

Fotini Papadopoulou and Penelope Konstandoudi[19]

Using technology they had learned both at the university and from their former employers, these two chemical engineers borrowed 20,000 drahkmai from their relatives and created their own laboratory, "Gnomodotis," specializing in water and soil analysis in Veria, Greece. They provide farmers with information and advice on how to improve yields and select fertilizers, targeting small and medium-sized farms that have yet to benefit from technological progress and that are too small to be worthwhile customers for the major laboratories. According to them, "Innovation is a continuous learning process which has its satisfactions. It expands one's knowledge and self-confidence."

Sometimes women become obsessed with an idea and can't rest until they have seen it through.

Elvire Neyret[20]

Elvire Neyret is a farmer who created "La Ferme du Bonheur," in the Nièvre region of France. She was unhappy with the fact that so many farm buildings are put to very little use while so many city-dwellers would like to have their children spend some time in the countryside. And so she designed her farm in a way that respects both people and animals and is suited to urban people's needs. Now at her farm she takes in problem children that have been sent on countryside holidays as a form of therapy. There she teaches them about plant and animal life. She is becoming an entrepreneur while also fulfilling her dream.

Finally, there are women who start from a clear vision of what their neighborhood's needs are, and who decide to meet them by starting a firm. Usually their goal is to encourage women to solve certain social problems.

Michèle Lecomte[21]

Take the case of Michèle Lecomte, the wife of a fisherman in Normandy, France. Her aim is to organize fishermen's wives to address the adverse trends in the fishing industry. She plans to do so by making information available about the situation of self-employed fishermen and the opportunities open to them. Now she works with partners from other European countries such as Portugal, Greece, Denmark, and Scotland. She has created an information-exchange network and publishes the newsletter *L'Enjourie*, "la voix des femmes à travers l'Europe." The newsletter reinforces local and international solidarity between women. She also organized training courses in the hardest-hit areas and a sailmakers workshop. She says, "My aim is to reach out to seafarers of all nationalities, through their wives, and make them understand the vital role women do play and should be encouraged to play."

These examples show the potential for innovation underlying feminine culture. In creating their own firms, women entrepreneurs did not start from a mathematical calculation of how much could be invested and how much could be earned in some business. They have started from a need that they felt was unmet. It was often a social need. They have tended to approach marketing in an innovative way: They created new markets providing services that didn't exist before. It is mainly through observation that innovators discover and develop the idea for a project.

Women entrepreneurs retain their lively curiosity as well as a desire to explore any opportunities for development. This has the huge advantage of making them adaptable to change, but mindful of others and concerned to maintain a balance among the clearly perceived forces and interests involved. As a result, women tend to prefer working in partnership with others. Women entrepreneurs are particularly conscious of the resistance their action may encounter and therefore place great emphasis on pooling experience and working in association with others as a means of avoiding possible hostility and conflict. The "Mappa del Tempo" project, for instance, was set up by a group of fourteen women who had met during a training course on tourism in Italy. Their association now offers a range of tours to suit those with an interest in history but who also want to meet people engaged in farming and food production. Their success didn't stop them from being very cautious. As they point out, "launching and running a business calls for determination and conviction."[22]

Difficulties are numerous because, besides those that any entrepreneur meets, women who want to start a firm have to cope with the particularly difficult aspect of being relative newcomers on the economic scene.

Monica Zeegers[23]

Monica Zeegers, 32, from Wychen, the Netherlands, has set up her own innovative firm in the sector of services for funerals. She provides a kind of funeral where black is not the dominant color, and she is very attentive to individual needs, even supplying the moral support and practical information so necessary at such times. She says, "You must take time to develop the idea before going into business. Make sure it is sound and test it out. Know what you want and be sure about it. If you do have doubts, always look into them to see if they are justified."

These stories may suggest that there is a special feminine culture of entrepreneurship: highly aware of their special needs and of the needs of their society, oriented to providing services that answer a previously unrecognized market demand, open to partnerships and very cautious. Of course, in the past there was no tradition of women entrepreneurs, and this creates special difficulties and opportunities. What seems to be certain is that women entrepreneurs give new possibilities to economies coping with unemployment. Economies wanting to explore these possibilities and able to understand the social and economic problems facing women entrepreneurs can also achieve a more general goal: They can progress along the path of modernization.

Modernization and the percentage of women entrepreneurs go together: They tend to strengthen one another. Traditional market regulations, barriers to information and financing, old ways of doing business are challenged by modernization and they are also major obstacles to the rise of women entrepreneurs. It is a trend that is particularly easy to observe in some Mediterranean countries, which are experiencing both rapid modernization and industrialization.

"During the last 25 years, Spanish society has seen a major change in every aspect of economic and social life," says Marina Subirats Martori, director of the Spanish Women's Institute. "This change has created a more favorable context for women."[24] The spread of education and the growth of the service sector have proved to be very important for everybody but particularly for women entrepreneurs: because while education produced a group of women more aware of their potential, the service sector has provided new opportunities for them. The number of firms led by women grew from under 10 percent in 1984 to 16 percent in 1993. Most of those firms were small: 88 percent of the enterprises had fewer than five employees and only 1 percent had more than fifty, compared with 2.4 percent of companies owned by men. Generally speaking, most of the women entrepreneurs had an average education, but the proportion of women entrepreneurs who had attended a university was higher than the corresponding figure for men. Their success is evident from the fact that the number of women entrepreneurs grew more rapidly than the number of men during the recovery of 1984–1989 and fell more slowly during the recession of 1990–1993. They were mostly involved in the textile and food sectors and in services with a particularly strong presence in retail, tourism, and education, and in various forms of assistance to enterprises. "Women entrepreneurs in Spain seem to go into business in both the traditionally feminine sectors and the new services to firms," concludes Subirats Martori.[25] In other words, they take advantage of the modernization but they also support it.

For too long, women's participation in the labor market has been considered secondary to that of men. Their potential to contribute to the process of economic growth has been largely ignored. This point of view no longer makes social, political, or economic sense. Women have experience, skills, ideas, and motivation to contribute to work and enterprise culture. Financial programs designed specifically for women can be useful in certain cases. Collecting more and better data on women's business ownership also has a very clear importance. Developing and promoting new images of women business ownership is another promising means of development.

In other words, special efforts for women are necessary: "In order to encourage entrepreneurship among women effectively," says Daniela Bertino, of the Office of International Technology (OIT), Turin, Italy, "there is a need to help prepare and implement a general strategy to support small businesses, while ensuring that such an action is conducted with a gender approach, supporting projects specifically intended for women."[26]

The most important general policies to address unemployment will be useful for both women and men: "To deal with unemployment means to answer the following question: How can a neighborhood join the mainstream of the local economy? This leads to linking together education, finance and infrastructure," says David Cragg, chief executive of the Birmingham Training and Enterprise Council, United Kingdom.[27] Christopher Brooks, director of the ILE Programme of the OECD, adds: "Governments organized a very strong system for providing infrastructures. Now we need a similar system to be built to provide intermediation between small firms and the various organizations that offer services like credit and education. Women will benefit just like anybody else. But we ought to bet on small business: It will not make things perfect for everybody, but it will make things better for many."[28] "Moreover, if women would like to build a modern and supportive society, to influence present and future policies, they should rely on innovation, based on strategic approaches such as creating networks and synergies between themselves and among decision makers, businesses and individuals at all levels," reminds Geneviève Lecamp, administrator at the OECD.[29]

"Fostering entrepreneurship and job creation among women," Lecamp says, "is by no means segregational, but follows, it seems to me, the obvious but neglected route to involving rural and urban communities in grasping opportunities driven and created by the changing conditions of producing and delivering goods and services. Equal opportunities do not have to apply exclusively to one gender in the future, but more broadly to all those who face difficulties in responding to whatever challenge with talent and imagination."[30]

Lillian Vernon

Lillian Vernon is probably one of the most widely regarded and respected female entrepreneurs in the industrialized world. For women looking for inspiration, her story is worth telling again, in her own words:

"In 1951, as a young bride, I launched the company that would become Lillian Vernon Corporation from the yellow Formica kitchen table in our apartment in Mount Vernon, a pleasant suburb of New York City. My goal was simple: I needed to supplement my husband's weekly pay of $75 from his family's dry-goods store. So, too, was my business plan: What I decided to sell was a handbag and a belt designed for teen-age girls.

"I gambled $2,000 of our wedding-gift money to place a one-sixth-of-a-page advertisement, which cost $495, in the September issue of *Seventeen* magazine. My gimmick was that the items could be monogrammed with as many as two initials. A week later, I wondered nervously if I had gotten an order. My husband checked the address I had given in the ad. "No," he said. "You got fifty."

The rest is history. With those first fifty orders, I had started a business that would eventually become a major specialty catalog retailer with annual revenues of $240 million. What I didn't realize at the time was that I, too, had been transformed: I had become an entrepreneurial businesswoman.

"In the early days, I didn't think much about being a female entrepreneur. Starting my own company was something I did because I had to: There was virtually no other way for a woman to earn a living wage in the jobs open to them 47 years ago. Yet I quickly learned there were complications. Many men were condescending and patronizing. When I shopped for merchandise at trade fairs, suppliers would often ask, "Are you buying for a gift shop?" My feelings of annoyance and outrage were tempered only by the knowledge that I would soon be out-grossing them all!

"A more serious obstacle was that women entrepreneurs—then a rarity, to say the least—were frequently denied credit. Once, when I asked for a short-term loan to order extra shipping cartons in a hurry, I was told, "Not possible." On another occasion, when I desperately needed extra space and didn't have the cash for the security deposit, I resorted to using as collateral for a bank loan some World War II bonds from my safety-deposit box!

Much has changed for today's burgeoning number of female entrepreneurs. For one thing, high-profile role models abound, among them Martha Stewart, Oprah Winfrey, and Warnaco Chief Executive Linda Wachner. For another, yesterday's near-taboo against having both a career and a family—which I also did in the 1950s—has virtually collapsed.

"To detractors who still say women can't have both, I say that if I did it then, women can surely do it now. Women's extensive experience and invaluable skill in dealing with multiple distractions and juggling many responsibilities equips them to be superb managers. In my case, what also helped was that I drew a line between where my business day ended and where my family time began. No matter how busy my days were, I always made sure I was home in the evening for my husband and sons.

"Today's women can more easily "have it all" as entrepreneurs. While men might occasionally condescend to them—let's face it, there are still jerks out there!—men are nonetheless apt to think twice. They could be talking to their future boss! With so many women in senior-level banking jobs, female entrepreneurs who do their homework don't have any trouble getting credit. Attitudes about a woman's "place" have changed dramatically. Best of all, role models have proliferated for today's generation.

"In my recent autobiography, *An Eye for Winners*, I attempted to share my experiences, both good and bad, because I believe that I am one of those role models. It is my hope that today's fledgling female business owners dispense with the old-fashioned myth that "a woman's place is in the home" and join the cadre of those daring to reach for their dreams."[31]

Although the vast majority of the tens of millions of women around the world who start businesses will never become household names like Lillian Vernon, the innumerable contributions they make to lives of their families, their communities, and their nations must surely be noted. In many ways, women entrepreneurs are pioneers who are leading us all into a new world, a new world full of greater opportunities for more individuals than ever before.

NOTES

1. Diane Starcher, "Women Entrepreneurs: Catalysts for Transformation," *UNDEP Quarterly*, (Fall 1999).

2. Ibid.

3. David Woodruff, "A Woman's Place is in Her Own Business," *Business Week*, March 18, 1996.

4. Ibid.

5. OECD member countries are virtually all the developed or industrialized countries in the world: Australia, Austria, Belgium, Canada, Denmark,

Finland, France, Germany, Greece, Iceland, Ireland, Italy, Japan, Luxembourg, the Netherlands, New Zealand, Norway, Portugal, Spain, Sweden, Switzerland, Turkey, the United Kingdom, and the United States.

6. Candida Brush, "The Irresistible Rise of Female Entrepreneurs," *Innovation and Employment*: OECD 14 (December 1993).

7. U.S. Small Business Administration Annual Statistical Report 1999.

8. Canadian Center for Small Business Development, Toronto, 1999.

9. Omar Sacirby, "German Women Create Their Jobs By Starting Their Own Businesses," *Christian Science Monitor*, March 13, 1998.

10. Ibid.

11. "The Rise of Women Entrepreneurs," from the United Nations Development web site, www.undep.org.

12. Ibid.

13. Starcher, "Women Entrepreneurs: Catalysts for Transformation."

14. Ibid.

15. "The World's Women 2000: Trends and Statistics," United Nations Department of Social Affairs, 2000.

16. Ibid.

17. Starcher, p. 00.

18. "The Rise of Women Entrepreneurs," www.undep.org.

19. Ibid.

20. Ibid.

21. Ibid.

22. Ibid.

23. Ibid.

24. Ibid.

25. Ibid.

26. Ibid.

27. Ibid.

28. Ibid.

29. Ibid.

30. Ibid.

31. This letter from Lillian Vernon is posted on the Internet at the Web site of the U.S. Small Business Administration, www.sba.gov.

2

Women and Globalization

It is good to swim in the waters of tradition but to sink in them is suicide.

Mahatma Gandhi

Every July, the southeastern United States makes its annual preparations for the hurricane season. Homeowners brush away the cobwebs to make sure their plywood supply is in order. Local governments tirelessly run over again and again the contingencies in their emergency response programs. American Red Cross offices stage mock drills in order to test the effectiveness of their relief plans. Insurance companies send additional agents to their Atlanta and Charlotte offices to be ready for the mountain of claims sure to follow. Meteorologists, aided by new developments in satellite technology, stand at the ready to predict where and when the hurricanes are likely to hit. Yet, with all of this preparation, high technology, and valuable information, hurricanes inevitably destroy property and devastate thousands of lives each year.

Like the annual hurricane season, the same can be said of the economic integration of humankind. To prepare themselves for the coming storm of "globalization," workers learn new skills that they believe will make them more employable. Governments make public policy that they hope will prepare their nation for the next turndown

Table 2.1
Gender Poverty Ratio, 2000, Selected Countries

COUNTRY	Women per Men Below the Poverty Line
Egypt	1.94
Ethiopia	2.23
Nigeria	2.69
South Africa	1.56
Uganda	1.79
Brazil	1.99
Colombia	1.95
Mexico	1.89
Panama	2.33
Peru	1.78
Poland	1.55
Russia	1.78
Ukraine	1.23
Uzbekistan	2.21
Bangladesh	2.24
China	1.03
India	2.76
Malaysia	1.65
Pakistan	2.46
Philippines	2.76
South Korea	1.33
Thailand	1.65
Australia	1.34
Canada	1.28
France	1.29
Japan	1.06
United Kingdom	1.19
United States	1.41

Source: WHO database; Johns Hopkins Population Information Program.

in GDP. Nongovernmental organizations like the United Nations try to anticipate which flash point will be the next one to require their assistance. Corporate leaders endeavor to predict which country or region will bring the highest profits. Economists, armed with more and more "real time" data, attempt to forecast which economy will be most affected by events in another.

All the same, when the next storm arises, tragedy inevitably strikes. Workers never seem to have the right skills. Governments appear to flounder. Nongovernmental organizations look overwhelmed. Corporations incredibly complain that local issues are preventing them from making a profit. As usual, economists scream for more data. All the while, the financial markets continue their slash-and-burn tactics in order to satisfy their insatiable appetite for easy and fast money.

Blatantly put, hardly anyone really knows what is going on. Nevertheless, the storm over the world's population continues to churn. Confidence is lost and currencies plummet. Investors pull their money out. Governments collapse. Multinationals, who days before were liquid, are nearly bankrupted.[1]

For hundreds of millions of women around the world, the situation is particularly confusing. The top decision-making positions that control globalization are still overwhelmingly occupied by men—primarily from developed countries. According to the *New York Times*, men hold about 90 percent of the top positions in major Wall Street investment firms. Men dominate the World Economic Forum (the annual meeting of global political and business leaders in Davos, Switzerland). Lists of speakers on the Web site of the forum held in January 2000 indicates that out of 392 panelists, less than 9 percent were women.

At the World Trade Organization (WTO) women are also in the minority. The World Bank is a little better: women constitute 36 percent of the key professional positions and almost 20 percent of the managerial and senior technical positions. At the International Monetary Fund (IMF), in contrast, a mere 11 percent of economists are women and only 15 percent of all managerial positions are held by women. These are the international financial institutions charged with managing globalization so as to promote stability, growth, and development. The above-mentioned human resource numbers beg the following question: Whose stability, whose growth, and whose development?

THE GLOBAL CONDITION OF WOMEN

The condition of women in light of globalization is even more obvious when we look at some key indicators of the status of women.

The phrase "feminization of poverty"[2] alludes precisely to the disproportionate representation of women among the poor, as compared to men (see Table 2.1). There are four basic elements to the concept of feminization of poverty:

1. A prevalence of women among the poor
2. The not fortuitous gender-biased impact of female poverty

3. The progressive increase in the disproportionate representation of wom-
   en among the poor
4. The degree of low visibility of female poverty

There are many reasons for the feminization of poverty. A society's
attitudes toward women can deny them access to the natural resources, credit, technology, and training that they need to run their
businesses. Women in many societies cannot travel as freely as men
and may be limited in the assets they can own. They are at a disadvantage when competing with those who have greater access to markets and new technology.

Globalization of the world economy also affects women's poverty.
Small woman-run businesses often can't compete with cheap imported products brought in by trade liberalization. In Africa, many
of women's traditional industries such as food processing and bas-
ketmaking are being wiped out. New employment opportunities have
been created in some parts of Asia, but often with low wages and
poor working conditions.

Traditional approaches to economic development have done little
to help. On the contrary, the number of rural women living in absolute poverty has risen by 50 percent over the last two decades (as
opposed to 30 percent for men).[3]

DISCRIMINATION

Discrimination begins at home with the undervaluing of domestic
duties because they don't directly generate income. When this unpaid
work is taken into account, women usually work more hours per week
than men do.

Not acknowledging "women's work" is particularly insulting in the
Third World, where women also do most of the agricultural work.
An African peasant woman might typically put in a sixteen-hour day
trudging long distances fetching firewood, animal fodder, and water;
growing and harvesting food; tending cash crops; and cooking and
caring for her family. Not surprisingly, this punishing routine leaves
little time or energy to look after her health or to seek education and
training—the very things that enable women to break the cycle of
low status and poverty.

Despite their pivotal role in agriculture, women rarely have property rights and so are seldom consulted about the land or included in
agricultural training programs. One result of this situation is envi-

Table 2.2
Women As Household Heads, 2000, by Region

	% of women who are heads of households
AFRICA	
Northern Africa	12
Sub-Saharan Africa	31
LATIN AMERICA	
Central America	22
South America	22
Caribbean	36
ASIA	
Eastern Asia	22
South-Eastern Asia	19
Southern Asia	9
Central Asia	24
Western Asia	10
OCEANIA	15
DEVELOPED REGIONS	31

Source: Statistics Division of the United Nations Secretariat, from *Women's Indicators and Statistics Database*, version 4.

ronmental degradation: because women lack the resources needed to improve their farms' productivity, the land—and the families living on it—suffer.

Many women now face the added burden of running households by themselves. Globally, a third of all households are headed by women, as migration in search of work or divorce removes husbands from the household (see Table 2.2).

Legal restraints on access to credit or landownership prevent them from improving their precarious situation and contribute to making these single-parent households the poorest of the poor.

LACK OF EDUCATION AND SKILLS

Lack of education and skills frequently forces women into the risky informal economy as street traders, domestic servants, homeworkers, and seasonal laborers. Although economically productive to society, once again this work is rarely recognized in official statistics and the women often get no protection from unions or employment legislation.

In Asia, more and more young women have been joining the official workforce in recent years and are experiencing some of the benefits—financial independence, higher status, and lower fertility rate through delaying the age of marriage. Children benefit also because women usually devote more of their income to the family's welfare than do men.

Just as women's domestic work is undervalued, so too are their skills in the world of employment. Most are concentrated in the poorly paid, low-skilled "women's" sectors of the economy, such as the free trade zones set up in many developing countries to attract foreign companies. Exhausting eighteen-hour days in unsafe and unhealthy conditions are the norm, along with sexual harassment and lack of job security. (See Tables 2.3 and 2.4a and b.)

The poor status of many of the world's women condemns them to equally poor health throughout their lives (see Table 2.5). In some countries, discrimination actually starts in the womb. India's Maharashtra state, for example, has banned ultrasound testing for sex determination because female fetuses were being aborted. The reason— the heavy dowry a couple is expected to pay when the girl is married. By the time they reach five, girls' infant mortality in India and Bangladesh can be double that of boys because, in allocation of food and health care, boys get most of the attention. In India, for instance, figures show that boys are breast-fed longer than girls and are taken for medical treatment more promptly.

The discrimination continues into adulthood, and so it is no surprise that energy-sapping anemia, a result of malnutrition, is a serious health problem for an estimated 250 million women, particularly in pregnancy.

Childbearing brings other problems. Poor people often have large families because children can work from an early age and then look after parents in later years. The resulting pattern of repeated childbearing and short intervals between births and pregnancy at an early age poses high risks to women's—and children's—health. (See Tables 2.6 and 2.7.)

Family planning services can help, yet in 1990 nearly 400 million women lacked access to basic contraception. More fundamentally, poor women must desire these services in the first place. This usually only happens when better education, health, and employment predisposes them to want smaller families.

AIDS poses an enormous threat to women. Worldwide, the disease is growing faster among women than among men. In some parts of the world, however, it is so unacceptable for women to take the initiative in sexual relationships that many dare not bring up the subject of safe sex, even with husbands. Women remain "faithful but fearful."

Table 2.3
Distribution of Female Labor Force, 2000, by Region

	Self-Employed	Wage and Salaried	Family Workers
AFRICA			
Northern Africa	10	62	28
Sub-Saharan Africa	27	30	43
LATIN AMERICA			
Central America	28	63	9
South America	31	58	9
Caribbean	15	81	4
ASIA			
Eastern Asia	8	81	9
South-Eastern Asia	25	53	22
Southern Asia	20	36	44
Central Asia	22	48	30
Western Asia	8	54	38
OCEANIA	19	41	40
DEVELOPED REGIONS	11	87	2

Source: Statistics Division of the United Nations Secretariat, *Key Indicators of the Labor Market*, 1999.

Table 2.4a
Women's Share of the Labor Force by Sector, 1998, by Region

	agriculture - women % total	industry - women % of total	services - women % of total
AFRICA			
Northern Africa	30	21	48
Sub-Saharan Africa	65	7	28
LATIN AMERICA			
Central America	8	12	73
South America	5	13	81
Caribbean	6	18	80
ASIA			
Eastern Asia	14	23	63
South-Eastern Asia	46	13	41
Southern Asia	66	18	15
Central Asia	42	14	43
Western Asia	21	16	63
OCEANIA	16	12	56
DEVELOPED REGIONS	4	13	38

Source: Statistics Division of the United Nations Secretariat, *Key Indicators of the Labor Market,* 1999.

Table 2.4b
Women's Share of the Labor Force, 1980–97, by Region

	1980 - % of labor force who are women	1997 - % of labor force who are women
AFRICA		
Northern Africa	20	26
Sub-Saharan Africa	42	43
LATIN AMERICA		
Central America	27	33
South America	27	38
Caribbean	38	43
ASIA		
Eastern Asia	40	43
South-Eastern Asia	41	43
Southern Asia	31	33
Central Asia	47	46
Western Asia	23	27
OCEANIA	35	38
DEVELOPED REGIONS	45	45

Source: Statistics Division of the United Nations Secretariat, *Key Indicators of the Labor Market*, 1999.

Table 2.5
Health Metrics for Women, 2000, Selected Countries

COUNTRY	Life Expectancy at Birth for Women	% of Pregnant Women Who Received Prenatal Care
Egypt	68	53
Ethiopia	44	20
Nigeria	52	60
South Africa	58	89
Uganda	40	87
Brazil	71	74
Colombia	74	83
Mexico	76	71
Panama	76	72
Peru	71	64
Poland	77	95
Russia	73	93
Ukraine	74	94
Uzbekistan	71	90
Bangladesh	58	23
China	72	79
India	63	62
Malaysia	74	90
Pakistan	65	18
Philippines	70	83
South Korea	76	96
Thailand	72	77
Australia	81	99
Canada	82	99
France	82	98
Japan	83	98
United Kingdom	80	97
United States	80	92

Source: Population Division of the United Nations Secretariat, *Women's Indicators and Statistics Database,* version 4.

Table 2.6
Adolescent Fertility Rates, 2000, by Region

	Births per 100 Women aged 15-19, Year 2000
AFRICA	
Northern Africa	44
Sub-Saharan Africa	130
LATIN AMERICA	
Central America	102
South America	67
Caribbean	57
ASIA	
Eastern Asia	12
South-Eastern Asia	40
Southern Asia	85
Central Asia	37
Western Asia	54
OCEANIA	62
DEVELOPED REGIONS	28

Source: Statistics Division of the United Nations Secretariat, from *Women's Indicators and Statistics Database*, version 4.

Table 2.7
Estimated Births per Woman, 1995–2000, by Region

	1995 - Births per Woman	2000 - Births per Woman
AFRICA		
Northern Africa	3.9	3.4
Sub-Saharan Africa	5.5	5.2
LATIN AMERICA		
Central America	4.1	3.7
South America	3.2	2.9
Caribbean	2.5	2.3
ASIA		
Eastern Asia	2.0	1.8
South-Eastern Asia	3.6	3.2
Southern Asia	4.7	4.3
Central Asia	3.7	3.3
Western Asia	4.3	3.8
OCEANIA	4.0	3.7
DEVELOPED REGIONS	1.7	1.6

Source: Statistics Division of the United Nations Secretariat, from *Women's Indicators and Statistics Database*, version 4.

Unequal access to education consigns many women to lives of low status and large families. Their inability to read the instructions on a packet of contraceptive pills or a pesticide container, a seed catalog or an invoice, a wage slip or a newspaper, excludes women from the full benefits of development and from making their full contributions as citizens. Despite this, illiterate women still manage to make outstanding contributions toward improving their lives and those of other women.

Women are at a grave disadvantage educationally in many parts of Asia and Africa, despite removal of formal barriers to school enrollment in most countries. In South Asia in 1987 there were only 73 girls for every 100 boys at primary level and 57 per 100 at secondary level. The ratios for tertiary and vocational training are even lower.

Not surprisingly, illiteracy is a major problem: Women make up almost two-thirds of illiterate adults in the developing world.

This reflects a continuing belief that there is little benefit in educating a girl when she could be working in the marketplace or fields. (Boys are affected by this thinking, too, though not to the same extent.)

Women who are shortchanged in this way pass the disadvantages on to their children. It has been estimated that in developing countries a child's mortality risk declines by an average of 7 to 9 percent for each extra year the mother is educated.

Better-educated mothers also tend to have smaller families, and this also benefits children. Studies in Thailand have shown that as the number of children per family drops, the proportion sent to school rises.

VIOLENCE AND INTIMIDATION

Women face physical violence and intimidation on many levels. For example, women and their children make up three-quarters of the world's refugees, fleeing persecution and war. This leaves them vulnerable to the sort of brutal rape and abduction experienced by the Vietnamese "boat women," who fled the war in Vietnam to several nations across Southeast Asia.

Women also suffer when arms spending by governments chews up precious funds that should be going toward social services for themselves and their children. In some of the poorest countries, such as Pakistan, military spending is at least twice that on health services and education.

Domestic violence and sexual harassment in the workplace are common in both developing and developed countries. Women work-

Table 2.8
Prevalence of Violence Against Women by an Intimate Partner,
Selected Countries

COUNTRY	Year	% of Adult Women Assaulted by Intimate Partner
Egypt	1996	34.4
Ethiopia	1995	45.2
Nigeria	1993	31.4
South Africa	1998	13.2
Uganda	1996	41.1
Brazil	1997	34.6
Colombia	1995	19.8
Mexico	1996	27.5
Panama	1996	9.5
Peru	1997	30.9
Poland	1998	14.9
Russia	1998	27.6
Ukraine	1997	29.8
Uzbekistan	1997	20.3
Bangladesh	1993	42.5
China	1998	18.4
India	1998	42.3
Malaysia	1998	16.3
Pakistan	1997	26.8
Philippines	1997	15.1
South Korea	1998	38.3
Thailand	1998	20.2
Australia	1998	8.1
Canada	1999	19.1
France	1999	12.2
Japan	1998	8.7
United Kingdom	1998	30.3
United States	1999	22.1

Source: WHO database; Johns Hopkins Population Information Program.

ers are regularly harassed in Mexico, according to trade union officials, while more than 50 percent of Pakistani wives report being beaten by their husbands. (See Table 2.8.)

Many poor women are also forced into prostitution to support themselves and their parents and children. Thousands of Thai women and young girls face the daily menace of rape, beatings, and sometimes murder in this dangerous occupation. Practices like female circumcision, early childhood marriage, and nutritional taboos continue to threaten women. For instance, female circumcision (genital mutilation might be a more appropriate term) still commonly occurs in parts of Africa and elsewhere and continues to menace at least 80 million women and young girls.

THE NATURE OF GLOBALIZATION

The inevitable economic integration of the world's people through globalization has been marked by moments of fantastic expansion as well as deep retrenchment. Most of the twentieth century may best be remembered as a retreat from the economic integration of the previous era. The isolationism of World War I, the despair of the Great Depression, and the horrors of World War II temporarily pushed back the march of Global Manifest Destiny in the first half of the century. Only within the last few decades have we been able to approach the levels of commerce that existed in the 1880s and 1890s. Freer world trade led to an explosion of American exports in 1896. In that year, American exports soared to 7 percent of the gross national product. In 1938 the number had fallen to 4 percent. By 1998 it was 8 percent.

The fervent nationalism that climaxed in World War I was building for two generations across Europe. The destruction caused by the world's first total war would provide the foundations for the next global war just twenty years later. During this time, the rapid economic integration of the pre-war years would suffer an enormous setback.

The period of the Great Depression, from the early 1930s until the arrival of World War II, witnessed an astonishing implosion of global trade and economic integration. Between 1929 and 1932 the value of world trade fell by a full 50 percent. Though deflation contributed to the loss in value, even at constant prices the volume of world trade in 1932 was nearly 30 percent below its 1929 level. As late as 1938, trade volume was still barely 90 percent of that in 1929, despite the near complete recovery of the production of primary products and manufactured goods.

Adding to this decline was a dramatic shift in the direction and pattern of economic integration. Trade and the flow of capital constricted from its multilateral constructs and was channeled into self-contained regional and colonial blocs such as the British Commonwealth, a group of European gold-standard countries centered in France, a Central European trade bloc linked to Germany, and a group of Western Hemisphere countries trading with the United States.

Even more than the cataclysm of World War I and the upheaval of the Great Depression, World War II shaped the current structure of global economic power. The ending of the colonial system, the worldwide presence of the Soviet Union, and the preeminence of the United States were all direct results of World War II. The shift in global hegemony away from Europe caused a retrenchment in the global economy that still has not regained the ground it held in the nineteenth century.[4]

Still, today's advance toward economic integration may very well touch many more people—especially women—than nineteenth-century commerce did.

THE IMPACT OF GLOBALIZATION ON WOMEN'S LIVES

Like men, most of the world's economically active women are operating in the informal sector producing goods that are often extremely sensitive to external competition. Many millions of women are linked indirectly to the international market through small sub-contracted workshops or as piece-based homeworkers to export industries. Firms like these are known as SMEs (small to medium-sized enterprises).

Woman-owned SMEs dominate in sectors such as agriculture, textiles, and clothing that are becoming more closely integrated into the global trading system. Still, women entrepreneurs often lack the same access as men to credit, training, technology, and information that is necessary to take advantage of new economic opportunities arising from trade liberalization.

Globalization has improved livelihoods, enabling the significant reduction in absolute poverty that has resulted. Globalization matches the productive capacity of the poor and underemployed (typically but not always low-skill labor, often female) with the physical location and labor needs of globalizing industries. For example, in Morocco, the incidence of poverty fell by half, from 26 percent to 13 percent of the population in just five years after trade was liberalized in the mid-1980s.

Countries that combine low wages with high technology skills have outcompeted more established countries. In just ten years, India has expanded its software development industry, centered on "Silicon Bangalore" to become the world's second-largest software exporter. In order to sustain and generalize the reduction in absolute poverty, the opportunity requires careful management.

Globalization can also increase inequality and be associated with labor conditions that use up the capabilities of the poor—by depleting health through poor working conditions, for example. Investment attracted by low wages alone can disappear as quickly as it materialized, leaving dislocated workers and structural unemployment in its wake. Woman-owned SMEs in Kenya and South Africa, making handicrafts and textiles and clothing, are finding their jobs being destroyed by cheaper imports from Asia. Woman-owned SMEs in South Korea are losing clothing jobs as South Korean firms relocate to cheaper areas of Asia.[5]

In many countries, it is the hinterland that is excluded from the global economy. Uneven regional development characterizes most economies and typically leads to the concentration of poverty in rural areas. In Africa, for example, the male population in rural areas is falling rapidly, while the female population remains relatively stable. In Malawi, the rural male population plummeted by 21.8 percent between 1970 and 1990. During the same twenty-year period, the rural female population declined by only 5.4 percent.

This trend has resulted in an increase in the proportion of households headed by women. Approximately one-third of all rural households in sub-Saharan Africa are now headed by women. Studies have shown that women heads of household tend to be younger and less educated than their male counterparts. They also generally have less land to work and even less capital and extra farm labor to work it with.

With a shortage of labor and capital, women heads of household are often forced to make adjustments to cropping patterns and farming systems. These adjustments have resulted in decreases in production and, in some cases, shifts toward less nutritious crops. Not surprisingly, these households often suffer from increased malnutrition and food insecurity.

In Southeast Asia, women provide up to 90 percent of labor for rice cultivation. In sub-Saharan Africa, women produce up to 80 percent of basic foodstuffs both for household consumption and for sale. Women perform from 25 to 45 percent of agricultural field tasks in Colombia and Peru. Women constitute 53 percent of the agricultural labor in Egypt. Fewer than 10 percent of women farmers in India, Nepal, and Thailand own land. An analysis of credit schemes in five African countries found that women received less than 10 percent of the amount of credit awarded to male smallholders.

As major providers of food and income, rural women are critical to the sustenance of the world's poor. In rural areas in developing

countries, women spend up to sixteen hours a day producing, processing, marketing, and preparing food, gathering fuel and water, and
performing other household tasks in addition to caring for their children and extended families. Most rural women are not directly re-
munerated for this work. A woman may work sixty hours or more a
week between domestic, farm, and off-farm tasks and yet receive no
wages or cash income of any kind. In fact, women in developing
countries work up to one-third more hours than men for an estimated
one-tenth of the income. Therefore, rural women confront a special
irony: They are overemployed in terms of hours worked and underemployed in terms of income received.

In war-torn Sierra Leone, several nongovernmental organization
(NGO) projects helped women farmers who had been displaced and
lost personal effects, farm tools, and seeds. Recognizing the very important role played by women in household food production, the
project distributed agricultural inputs including hand tools, fertilizer,
and seeds to 8,865 women, although it is estimated that 18,000
women benefited. In addition, 319 farmers, 158 extension staff, and
21 field staff from NGOs attended workshops, where they learned
better farming techniques.

The effects of migration to urban areas may also leave remaining
household members in absolute poverty. Among these, female-headed
households tend to form an identifiable group. While uneven regional
economic development is an old problem, globalization sharpens disparities and also offers new opportunities by opening new gateways.
In addition, it is clear that the interests, risks, and opportunities resulting from globalization affect different groups of women differently—what will benefit some women will have a negative impact on
others and will not affect yet others.

For example, the expansion of the ready-made garment industry in
Bangladesh led to the rural-to-urban migration of thousands of
young, usually single, women. Although working conditions are poor,
results from surveys of female garment workers show that the women
consider their alternatives to this employment—mainly domestic
service or agricultural labor—to be worse. While leaving much to be
desired, these women see expanding employment in this sector as a
definite opportunity.

The relatively poor, particularly women, are often found in the
service sector, which tends to be more labor-intensive. A challenge is
to devise ways in which these services can be connected with foreign

direct investment and with international markets, so that women can share in the benefits of the globalization process—especially as entrepreneurs.

Eugenia Kleiman and Martha Gámez[6]

For Eugenia Kleiman and Martha Gámez of Monterrey, Mexico, it began as a whim. "We wanted to build something beautiful, something different," said Kleiman, a former shoe shop owner. In 1990, she teamed up with Gámez, an interior designer, to create Margen Arteobjeto, a workshop that would make home furnishings from wrought iron.

Using personal savings, the two rented a small garage, hired a craftsman, and began displaying their plate holders and lampstands at regional fairs. Buyers were impressed, and orders began to trickle in. The products also caught the eye of an official from Bancomex, Mexico's export-promotion bank, who encouraged the pair to show their wares at trade fairs in the United States. Before long, major department stores were placing bulk orders.

"At first our U.S. customers were hesitant, because they had a bad image of Mexican producers," said Kleiman. "But we made it our business to erase that image through quality and service. Now our U.S. customers say, 'Why should we buy from Southeast Asia when you folks are right here?' "

By late 1996, Margen had grown to some 300 full-time employees operating in three round-the-clock shifts. Annual sales topped $8 million in 2000. Most recently, Margen was named one of the four most successful export-oriented companies in Mexico by Bancomex. Margen's story illustrates just how quickly entrepreneurs can germinate when the environment for growth is right.

There is no doubt that globalization leads to new risks and new vulnerabilities. However, where globalization is associated with new investment, new manufacturing production locations, new business opportunities for a large number of women, and additional demand for the paid labor of women, there are positive direct effects for women.

A strong, open economy, access to financing, transparent and efficient regulations, and effective legal protections: all these conditions must be present for female entrepreneurs to prosper over the long run.

Domitila Yupanqui[7]

When Domitila Yupanqui arrived in the Bolivian capital of La Paz, she hoped merely to survive. One of thousands of Bolivians who migrated to the city with nothing but the clothes on their backs after several state-owned mines in the province of Oruro were closed in the 1980s, Yupanqui had few contacts and no prospects.

"When we first moved to La Paz, we rented a single room," Yupanqui recalls. "I used to sell candy on the street. I would sit there, thinking about my children and their future, and feel very sad."

That was before Yupanqui heard about a bank that offered small short-term loans without requiring collateral. Intrigued, she inquired at the nearest branch of BancoSol, where to her surprise she was immediately treated as a potential customer. Told that she would need to form a small cooperative of fellow borrowers in order to qualify for a loan, Yupanqui recruited members for a group that called itself "the Cornfields."

Yupanqui used her first BancoSol loan to buy canned food. Since her vending stall was close to a public school, she used her second loan for school supplies. She continued to diversify, and by the time she had qualified for a fifth loan Yupanqui was able to rent a small storefront and begin selling electrical appliances. Today Yupanqui owns three stores and is paying to send two of her children to college.

Women make up half the world's human resources. This seemingly obvious fact has many dimensions, which must be viewed in the current global economic and social context. As industrialized nations struggle to achieve economic growth and job creation, human-resource management, creativity, and innovation are the cornerstones of an agenda for improved social and economic conditions.

All the world's nations are undergoing deep changes and are increasingly challenged by the globalization of markets, increased competition, and the growing interdependence of economies. At the same time, empirical evidence shows that woman-owned SMEs are an important source of employment generation, innovation, and economic development. This potential tends to remain largely undeveloped, however, and many policy challenges arise because of market imperfections, inappropriate policies, and institutional inconsistencies that discriminate against woman-owned SMEs.

Woman-owned SMEs are reported to be growing at a faster rate than the economy as a whole in several countries, but removing a number of obstacles would allow their potential to be fully tapped. Their contributions and needs must be examined, and the commensurate structural reforms applied.

Fostering the participation of women entrepreneurs in the process of globalization strengthens the economy and can be a source of political, economic, and social innovation. Women business owners' different vision of organization and management constitute a source of innovation in company structure, community service, and the use of technology. Because of these realities, we owe it to ourselves to promote and encourage woman-owned SMEs wherever and whenever we can.

NOTES

1. John A. Caslione and Andrew R. Thomas, *Growing Your Business in Emerging Markets: Promise and Perils* (Westport, Conn.: Quorum Books, 2000), pp. 1–2.

2. The phrase "the feminization of poverty" was coined in 1978 by Diana Pearce, a researcher at the University of Wisconsin.

3. Ibid.

4. Caslione and Thomas, p. 26.

5. Ibid.

6. George Psacharopoulos, ed., *Case Studies on Women's Employment and Pay in Latin America* (Washington, D.C.: World Bank, 1992), pp. 171–72.

7. Ibid., p. 276.

3

The Empowerment of Women

"Human progress, if not engendered, is endangered."
UN *Report on Women*, 1999.

The recognition of equal rights for women along with men, and the determination to combat discrimination on the basis of gender, are achievements equal in importance to the abolition of slavery, the elimination of colonialism, and the establishment of equal rights for racial and ethnic minorities.

Human development is a process of enlarging the choices for all people, not just for one part of society. Such a process becomes unjust and discriminatory if most women are excluded from its benefits. And the continuing exclusion of women from many economic and political opportunities is a continuing indictment of modern progress.

For too long, it was assumed that development was a process that lifts all boats—that its benefits trickled down to all income classes and that it was gender-neutral in its impact. Experience teaches otherwise. Wide income disparities and gender gaps stare us in the face in most societies.

Moving toward the true empowerment of women is not a technocratic goal—it is a political process. It requires a new way of thinking, in which the stereotyping of women gives way to a new philosophy that regards all people, irrespective of gender, as essential agents of change.[1]

The human development paradigm, which puts people at the center of its concerns, must thus be fully engendered. Any such attempt would embrace at least the following three principles:

- Equality of rights between women and men must be enshrined as a fundamental principle. Legal, economic, political, or cultural barriers that prevent the exercise of equal rights should be identified and removed through comprehensive policy reforms and strong proactive measures.
- Women must be regarded as agents and beneficiaries of change. Investing in women's capabilities and empowering them to exercise their choices is not only valuable in itself but is also the surest way to contribute to economic growth and overall development.
- The engendered development model, though aiming to widen choices for both women and men, should not predetermine how different cultures and different societies exercise these choices. What is important is that equal opportunities to make a choice exist for both women and men.[2]

In very few societies do women enjoy the same opportunities as men. Yet every country has made progress in developing women's capabilities. Across the globe, female life expectancy has increased 20 percent faster than male life expectancy over the past two decades. High fertility rates, which severely restrict the freedom of choice for women, have fallen by a third—from 4.7 live births per woman in 1970 to 3.0 in 1990. Life choices are expanding as women are progressively liberated from the burden of frequent childbearing and from the risk of dying in childbirth. Maternal mortality rates have been nearly halved in the past two decades.

More than half the married women of reproductive age in the developing world, or their partners, used modern contraceptives in 1990, compared with less than a quarter in 1980. This planned parenthood has brought women much greater control over their lives.

In adult literacy and school enrollment, the gaps between women and men were halved between 1970 and 1990 in developing countries. Women's literacy increased from 54 percent of the male rate in 1970 to 74 percent in 1990—and combined female primary and secondary enrollment increased from 67 percent of the male rate to 86 percent. Female rates of adult literacy and combined school enrollment in the developing world increased twice as fast as male rates between 1970 and 1990. Overall, female primary enrollment in developing countries increased 1.7 percent a year during 1970, compared with 1.2 percent for male enrollment. Girls' combined primary and secondary enrollment in the developing world jumped dramatically, from 38 percent in 1970 to 68 percent in 1992. East Asia (83 percent) and Latin America (87 percent) are already approaching the high levels of female school enrollment found in industrial countries (97 percent).[3]

It is still an unequal world. Among the developing world's 900 million illiterate people, women outnumber men two to one. Girls constitute the majority of the 130 million children without access to primary school. Poverty has a woman's face—of the 1.3 billion people in absolute poverty, the majority are women.[4]

WHAT IS EMPOWERMENT?

The term *empowerment* is found throughout development cooperation policy statements, documents, and information publications, but definitions are rare, and indicators to measure progress toward empowerment even rarer. In education alone, a computerized search recently yielded 2,900 scholarly entries applying to the term empowerment. Scarcely a problem exists—drug addiction, mental illness, sexual inequality, poverty, health care, racial strife—that has not attracted the nostrum of empowerment.

In 1993, for example, the U.S. government joined the crowd and embarked on a massive "Empowerment Zone" attempt to reenergize 106 cities and rural communities. Former president George Bush proclaimed "empowerment" the centerpiece of his domestic assistance program. A Yahoo search reveals some 221 empowerment organizations.

We have already learned that empowerment is not something that can be done by outsiders "to" people. Development cooperation initiatives are overly ambitious and doomed to fail if they seek to "empower women" themselves. Instead, these programs can help to create the conditions whereby women can become the agents of their own development and empowerment.

A key aspect of empowerment is women's participation in formal political structures. This was recognized in one of the critical areas of concern in the Beijing *Platform for Action*, "women in power and decision-making." When they signed this document, governments agreed to

• take measures to ensure women's equal access to and full participation in power structures and decision making

• Increase women's capacity to participate in decision making and leadership

According to one definition of an empowerment approach, it "questions some of the fundamental assumptions concerning the interrelationship between power and development. . . . it seeks to identify power less in terms of domination over others (with its implicit assumption that a gain for women implies a loss for men), and more in terms of the capacity of women to increase their own self-reliance and internal strength."[5] Other definitions of empowerment push further, arguing that empowerment for women implies the "radical alteration of the processes and structures which reproduce women's subordinate position as a gender."[6]

NGOs and women's organizations also assume a prominent place in many discussions of empowerment. Given the emphasis on women's own awareness, capacity development, and collective articulation of interests, NGOs appear to offer more potential to support empowerment than do state institutions. NGOs and women's organizations also have their weaknesses, and it is important to differentiate between organizations and to understand their strengths and limitations in contributing to empowerment.[7]

A useful concept introduced into the discussion of empowerment by Kate Young is that of "transformatory" potential.[8] The crucial element in transformatory thinking is the need to transform women's position in such a way that the advance will be sustained. Equally important is for those women themselves to feel that they have been the agents of the transformation, that they have won this new space for action themselves. It is also important that they realize that each step taken in the direction of gaining greater control over their lives will churn up other needs, other contradictions to be resolved in turn.

The assumption behind transformatory potential is that the process of women working together and solving problems on a trial-and-error basis, of learning by doing and also of learning to identify allies and forging alliances when needed, will lead to empowerment, both collective and individual.

Although some definitions of empowerment tend to focus on strengthening women's economic independence (through more income and greater individual self-reliance), a more useful approach appears to recognize the multiple roles and interests that women have and the interrelationships between them. Although there may be advantages to dividing women's lives into different roles, these pieces should always be put back together again to understand that women do not act and participate only as mothers or only as workers or only as activists.[9]

It is now more widely recognized that the problem is not a failure to integrate women into development or their lack of skills, credit, and resources, but the *social processes and institutions* that produce inequalities between women and men to the disadvantage of women. Inequalities between women and men are not only a cost to women but to development as a whole, and for that reason they must be conceived as societal and development issues rather than a "women's concern."

There are political as well as technical aspects that must be taken into account in addressing inequalities: It is not only a matter of "adding women in" to existing processes and programs, but of reshaping processes and programs to reflect the visions, interests, and needs of women and to support gender equality and empowerment.

WOMEN'S DEMANDS FOR EMPOWERMENT

It is disheartening that some societies still see advancement for women as a threat. The power of women's faith and vision moves necessary change forward, despite obstacles. Women will no longer be silenced, subdued, threatened, or persuaded to give up their right to a fair share of the planet. They are demanding to be empowered. Here are some examples:

- In Hong Kong, a "Women's Passion Show" used theater and personal testimonies to campaign against sex trafficking and "comfort women." It was one of the most attended productions in all Hong Kong during 1999.

- On May 8, 2000, from every corner of India, 150,000 women and children marched to protest child labor, economic injustice, poverty, and violence in New Delhi.

- Despite the continuous violence, Israeli and Palestinian women have successfully established a working partnership through a project of Jerusalem Link called "Women Making Peace." A similar dialogue is also taking form in Cyprus, encouraging a spirit of cooperation between Greek and Turkish communities there.

- In Yugoslavia, Zene u Crnom (Women in Black) has organized more than 100 peaceful demonstrations and silent vigils to protest Serbia's militarism, discrimination, and atrocities against civilians and to encourage cooperation. These women provide food and shelter to Kosovan refugees and treat

Albanian women like sisters. They were instrumental in the final collapse of the Milosevic regime.

• In Brazil, women living in the countryside marched more than 3,000 miles carrying 82 crosses inscribed with the names of murdered women.

• Afghan women denied many rights under the fundamentalist Islamic political and military force, the Taliban, formed the Revolutionary Association of Women of Afghanistan (RAWA) to defend against suffocating isolation, repression, physical attacks, and death threats. RAWA has been especially active in refugee camps, organizing schools and hospitals and conducting literacy, nursing, and vocational training courses for women.

• In Newcastle, Ontario, women posted three boxes around town to anonymously collect personal stories of poverty and abuse that will later be complied in a mural to portray the pain in their community and to spark change.

MEXICO

In Chiapas, Mexico, most of the displaced and poorest people are aboriginal women and children. Indigenous women are the main victims of acts of terrorism: physical and mental torture, rape, and forced migration by the army are part of their daily experience. These women have the highest rates of extreme poverty, illiteracy, and infant and maternal mortality in the country. Young women and girls are particularly vulnerable. The economic and political structures reinforce the problem of poverty and violence. It is now estimated that 80,000 soldiers are currently based in the state of Chiapas. There is rampant high-level corruption, racism, and sexism. It has become clear that law enforcement in Chiapas does not exist. As one woman says, "Our situation is so hard. . . . when our efforts are frustrated, it affects not only ourselves, but all other women and deeply hurts our families."[10]

"Indigenous women want to live, want to study, want hospitals and medicine and schools. We want food, respect, justice and dignity."[11] In November 1999, 5,000 indigenous and Mestizo women from 48 municipalities in the state of Chiapas participated in the Conference of Women United Against Violence, Impunity, and War in Chiapas. They condemned the violence rooted in war and unjust political and economic structures. Women spoke of the lifelong psychological effects of violence: the pain, grief, frustration, fear, and blame. Most important was the realization that all these women share the same problems despite different ethnic backgrounds. Their motivation is clear: "To regain our dignity, to recognize our reality, to write our own history, to reclaim our feminine selves, to make our own decisions."[12]

Guadalupe Buendia, a short, matronly woman who dresses modestly, is not someone you would imagine commanding power, let alone an army of 25,000 followers willing to take up arms and give their lives to follow her direction. But she is one of a handful of women who have achieved the nearly unthinkable in macho Mexican society: She has become a *cacique*, or chieftain, earning the nickname "la Loba"—She Wolf—for her toughness.

Buendia, 49, was recently arrested after her followers, perched on rooftops in the working-class city of Chimalhuacan outside Mexico City, opened fire on supporters of a rival *cacique* who won the local mayor's race after one of Buendia's sons was passed over as the candidate.

"In the case of poor urban zones, there is a new phenomenon by which men go to work and women stay back to guard the fort," said political analyst Lorenzo Meyer. "These are the women assuming leadership."[13]

In some cases, *caciques* command their people to take up arms and defend the interests of the leader. The brawl in Chimalhuacan, which left up to fifteen dead and several dozen wounded, has brought the female *cacique* into the public eye.

The influence of women bosses is growing and extends across social ranks in Mexico from teachers to garbage collectors, from street vendors to housekeepers. "The change in gender is what's new," Meyer said of the phenomenon, which has its origins in the pre-Hispanic era.

La Loba, who boasted to Mexico's *Milenio* magazine of having as many as 25,000 women supporters, is one of a host of powerful matriarchs who have emerged across the nation.

In March 1999 Silvia Sánchez, another middle-aged woman of apparently modest means, and thousands of her minions clashed with rival vendors in the nation's capital in a fight over who would sell their wares on the choicest streets.

Sánchez, who spent a year in jail on charges of theft and assault causing bodily harm, inherited her empire of some 12,000 vendors from her mother, Guillermina Rico, known as "La Jefa," or the Lady Chief, who died in 1997.

Guillermina de la Torre inherited the *cacique* crown from her late husband, a powerful merchant known as the "Garbage Czar." She and her son still control thousands of scavengers who sort garbage for items of value at one of the country's largest dumps.

Caciques provide their followers with everything from land and property to basic services such as water, electricity, and even jobs. Some go as far as arranging weddings and providing marriage counseling while others pay for funerals for the families of their followers.

"While the phenomenon of *caciques* is traditionally associated with land and property disputes, in Mexico it has also reached other sectors and groups," said Fernando Salmerón of the Center for Investigations and Superior Studies of Social Anthropology.[14] Leaders like Buendia break the mold of the Latin American *cacique*.

PHILIPPINES

The story is eerily similar in the Philippines. "It is enough that our nation withstood and suffered the horror of a fascist dictatorship for two decades. We will not allow [our] president to emulate an evil regime that we ousted thirteen years ago. In the most trying times, Filipino women never failed to stand together with the rest of the nation in protest. Let us now unite in the fight for democracy and against rising tyranny," reads a statement from Gabriela, a member organization of the National Alliance of Women's Organizations in the Philippines.[15]

The economic situation of the country under President Erik Estrada went from bad to worse to worst. Economic and political policies ignored the general population. People endured landlessness and job insecurity, as well as steady price increases in essentials like food, electricity, and oil. There was massive high-level corruption and money was channeled into militarization while education funding was cut. Maricel Gavina, youth chairperson for Gabriela, explains, "Due to poverty, more and more students are dropping out of school. Despite working on the side and our parents taking on extra paid work, we just cannot make ends meet. The government is not helping."[16]

Wages are purposely capped while police use force to dismantle strikes. Women are bearing the brunt of the turmoil. Nerrissa Guerrero, chairperson of the Concerned Mothers' League, explains, "We have been living in extremely dehumanizing situations. In order to cope we eat breakfast, lunch and dinner rolled into one meager meal a day or feed our families recycled food from fast-food waste."[17]

Given the increasing poverty and governmental corruption, about two thousand people leave the country every day. More than 7.2 million Filipino migrant workers live in 168 countries; the majority of the migrants are female. The desperation of poverty leaves them vulnerable to cheap labor, trafficking in girls and women, and a flourishing international sex trade.

Filipino women are demanding that policymakers make changes. "Filipino women have to forge international solidarity among the toiling women of the world in order to liberate us from oppression and exploitation. While the struggle of women's groups in every country is unique, the March unites them in the same struggle: to bring an end to the terrible poverty and violence most women face. Like women everywhere, we are using the March to launch a significant campaign to pursue a more just and humane society for our children!" according to Tess Agustin of PINAY, a Filipino women's organization in Canada.[18]

EMPOWERMENT AND FEMALE ENTREPRENURSHIP

Entrepreneurship is one of the best tactics within the strategic realm empowering women and elevating them to the equal status they are entitled to. What is needed is an environment that fosters women who desire to be entrepreneurs.

For billions of the world's women, life is a complex web of constraints, obligations, and sacrifices, many of which are determined from the day of their birth. The caste or ethnic group into which a woman is born determines her status and her degree of freedom. Group identify is just one element of status. Patriarchal family structures continue to dictate much of the course of a woman's life. Many women in developing countries have few options for survival other than getting married and producing children.

In some countries women are becoming more empowered to take control of their destinies. The vast majority of Nepali women are married early, often with little choice about who their partner will be. Because a woman eventually joins her husband's family anyway, parents do not feel obligated to invest in their daughters' education or development.

In rural areas particularly, Nepali girls and women work far more than boys and men, spending 25 to 50 percent more time on household tasks and economic and agricultural activities. A rural Nepali girl contributes to the livelihood of her household from a very young age. She fetches water, fodder, and firewood; tends to livestock and younger siblings; and helps her mother with housework and agricultural tasks. Although she bears many burdens both inside and outside her home, she is often fed after her brothers, discouraged from continuing her education, married off at an early age, not allowed to inherit any property, treated as an outsider in her husband's home, and in some very poor areas, deceived by promises of false jobs and sold into prostitution.

Women's participation in the formal economy is still a relatively new concept in Nepal. In 1991 about 45 percent of the female population (10 years and older) were recorded as economically inactive, despite the fact that Nepali women are the predominant productive force in the agricultural economy. Women also have primary responsibility for child care and other domestic chores. At the grassroots, control over scarce resources has traditionally been limited and women in particular have been excluded. Security of income is less for women than for men, because women lack individual ownership of assets, especially land.

Women who participate in the market economy can increase their status within the household and community. They are also more likely to participate in household decision making and to demand their legal rights. Research shows that women's access to and activity within the market economy results in a significant increase in their authority within the household and community. When women become empowered as entrepreneurs, there is a strong positive correlation with the education, health, and productivity of household members, particularly children. In short, things get a lot better.

TECHNOLOGY AND THE EMPOWERMENT OF FEMALE ENTREPRENEURS

Women must have the opportunity to benefit from the information technology revolution. As United Nations Development Programme (UNDP) Administrator Mark Malloch Brown declared in a public statement in May 1999, "information and communication technologies can do more to help the poor, the isolated and excluded, than nearly any other tools currently available."

Use of new information and communication technologies such as the Internet is one of the most important ways to reach the global market. Women owners of SMEs can now use computers to exchange information on supply and demand, market prices, and micro-credit and to market traditional handicrafts, textiles, and agricultural prod-

ucts. Already throughout the developing world, the Internet is proving its enormous potential for competing in local markets, and in the
global market as well. Information and communication technologies
can also promote critical social goals by enabling women and families
in remote regions to receive critical health and education services,
which they otherwise might not receive.

It is revealing to note that

- The radio took 38 years to be adopted by 50 million users
- The computer took 16 years
- The Internet needed only 4 years[19]

The Internet is making the world change faster than before, and these
changes will benefit all the world's women and help to empower
them.

For the woman entrepreneur, the Internet opens new business opportunities with higher growth rates. Research indicates that small
businesses that use the Internet have grown 46 percent faster than
those that do not.[20] These indicators are very favorable for woman-
owned firms, particularly those that have adopted technology. The
Internet and high-technology firms have created an environment of
advancement and opportunity for people in general worldwide.

Many Asian countries have started to encourage women to learn
computer and Internet skills. In Korea alone, 42 percent of all Internet users are women. And in the United States, the number of women
using the Web is growing faster than the number of men.

GLOBAL TRADE AND THE EMPOWERMENT OF
FEMALE ENTREPRENEURS

Trade policy and agreements, through the promotion of economic
development, can play an important role in increasing opportunities
and empowering women around the world. A clear lesson of the past
decades is that participation in trade and the world economy helps
countries to develop. Over the past fifty years, trade has been one of
the most dynamic forces for economic growth. In part, as a result of
trade agreements, which have substantially reduced tariffs and other
trade barriers worldwide, trade has expanded fifteenfold, economic
production has grown sixfold, and per capita income has nearly tri-
pled.

A number of recent studies from the UNDP and the World Trade Organization (WTO) conclude that openness to trade helps developing countries catch up with wealthier countries, and that those in poverty generally benefit from the faster-paced economic growth that trade liberalization brings. During the last fifty years, only one developing country, Botswana, has achieved rapid economic growth without rapid growth in manufacturing exports.[21]

On the other hand, history has shown us that nations that isolate themselves from trade tend to stagnate. As Southeast Asia, Central Europe, and Latin America opened to the world, they grew more rapidly, reduced poverty, and built more stable, peaceful regions. By contrast, South Asia, the Middle East, and Africa, where trade barriers remain highest, have reduced poverty more slowly. It is interesting to compare, for example, Asian and African economic policies of the past several decades. Thirty years ago, African per capita income generally was higher than Asian income. While many Asian countries pursued outward trade policies, African countries established very high trade barriers. The result was devastating for Africa, where disparities in the distribution of income have been the most extreme and per capita income is among the lowest in the world. Africa's share of world trade shrank during this period, depriving the continent of much needed revenues. Today, however, open trade and economic policies are being embraced by many African nations and we are seeing a new beginning for Africa.

Open trade promotes exports by making products more competitive and more affordable and leads to new and better-paying jobs. It also creates equal opportunities and a level playing field, particularly for small and medium-sized companies who might otherwise not be able to sell to export markets.

Open trade agreements also give people access to a wider choice of goods at lower prices, especially food, clothing, and other basic necessities, which account for the lion's share of expenses of the poor. For example, India's agreement to abolish import quotas meant that for the first time in fifty years, its vast population could have access to a wide range of affordable consumer goods. Open trade agreements also establish fair trading rules, helping to ensure that companies and workers are safeguarded against unfair trade practices.

Further, trade agreements and the world trading system give nations a greater stake in the stability and prosperity of their neighbors, which contributes to strengthening peace.

Trade can also play a significant role in empowering women in the developing world. As Hillary Rodham Clinton put it in her June 2000 speech to the United Nations General Assembly Session on Women, "women's progress depends upon economic progress." And experience has shown that trade and investment have been among the most effective means to bring about economic progress worldwide. Trade, therefore, is essential for development and can empower women. For successful development to occur, however, economic benefits must extend to women, who comprise approximately two-thirds of the world's poor.

Trade policy can create new opportunities but can never substitute for domestic policy or financial stability. Governments need to make public investments with particularly high social returns, especially girls' education and basic health services and immunization of all children. Governments must also promote an effective rule of law through good governance, transparency, and support for the emergence of a healthy civil society.

Experience also tells us that as important as the larger national economic policies may be, it is equally clear that where girls are unable to attend school, or women farmers and small business operators cannot find the credit to start businesses or the technologies that help them reach customers, development is slow and difficult. On the contrary, when girls are in school, when women with a good idea can find the credit to develop it and have the same access to telecommunications and computer networks that major companies enjoy as a matter of course, development is more rapid, stable, and sustainable.

Developed countries must ensure that the poorest countries enjoy the benefits of trade through programs that offer developing countries special duty-free access to their markets, such as the U.S. Generalized System of Preferences program, the Caribbean Basin Initiative, and the Africa Growth and Opportunity Act. They should also offer strong technical assistance and capacity-building programs that help less developed countries to become familiar with trade programs and agreements and assert their rights.

NOTES

1. Marilee Karl, *Women and Empowerment: Participation and Decision Making* (London: Zed Books, 1995).

2. Ibid.

3. Ibid.

4. Nalia Kabeer, "Empowerment from Below: Learning from the Grass-

roots," in Nalia Kabeer, ed., *Reversed Realities: Gender Hierarchies in Development Thought* (London: Verso, 1994).

5. Carolyn Moser, *Gender Planning and Development: Theory, Practice, and Training* (New York: Routledge, 1993).

6. Ibid.

7. Ibid.

8. Kate Young, *Planning Development with Women: Making a World of Difference* (London: Macmillan, 1993).

9. Ibid.

10. "Chiapas en Duda," *La Jornada* (Mexico City), May 21, 1999, p. 12.

11. Ibid.

12. Ibid.

13. Ibid.

14. Ibid.

15. Tony Tam, "Reducing the Gender Gap: How Important is Increasing Women's Experience," *World Development* 24, 5 (1996), p. 831.

16. "Women at the Forefront," *Philippines Star*, April 29, 2000.

17. Ibid.

18. Ibid.

19. From Tracy Wilens's speech at the Pacific Economic Cooperation Council Summit, San Francisco, Calif., November 2000.

20. Ibid.

21. John A. Caslione and Andrew R. Thomas, *Growing Your Business in Emerging Markets: Promise and Perils* (Westport, Conn.: Quorum, 2000), p. 20.

PART II

THE PARTICIPANTS

4

Women As Business Owners

Women and SMEs constitute the main weapons for helping us
to build a future without discrimination. We fight for our rights,
and not for privileges, because business has no gender.
Ms. Ann Diamantopoulou, Minister of Development, Greece

Without question, small and medium-sized enterprises (SMEs) are a
crucial source of employment, innovation, and economic development. Nevertheless, their potential tends to remain far from fulfilled.
This is particularly true for woman-owned SMEs, which are growing
at a faster rate than the economy as a whole in most countries of the
world. At the same time, the economic potential of women entrepreneurs remains partly untapped. The need to improve economic and
social performance today calls for looking more closely at the contributions and needs of woman-owned SMEs for three main reasons:

• *Economic*: Woman-owned SMEs are creating employment for themselves
and others. Many companies invest in their women staff members over a
long period but do not promote them to the highest levels of management
(the so-called glass ceiling). Thus, the economy has, in effect, invested in
these employees without ever seeing a full return on its investment. Providing opportunities to these women to branch out and create their own

firms is a way of capitalizing fully on the skills and training they have acquired.

• *Social*: In addition to helping women out of unemployment, enterprise creation offers women the flexibility to balance work and family responsibilities, since they manage their own time; the ability to support the family or supplement family income; and to serve as role models for their children. All this contributes to families which are better off and improves social cohesion.

• *Personal*: Running and owning an SME creates a greater degree of self-reliance, which enhances a woman's self-image. The autonomy enables the woman business owner to exercise more influence over the events of her own life.

Fostering the participation of women entrepreneurs strengthens the economy and can be a source of political, economic, and social innovation. Women business owners, in relation to their male counterparts, often have different demands on their time and different ways of seeing things and may be newer to the market. They therefore do business differently from men and, consequently, constitute a real potential source of innovation in terms of management style, company structure, services rendered to the community, and the use of technology.

WOMAN-OWNED BUSINESSES IN THE UNITED STATES

Between 1977 and 1999, the most recent years for which data is available from the U.S. Department of Commerce, the number of woman-owned businesses rapidly expanded by nearly 15 percent each year, while between 1972 and 1977 the number of woman-owned businesses remained relatively stable. The number of woman-owned businesses with paid employees grew at the slightly better rate of 16 percent each year between 1977 and 1999. By 1999 there were 6.8 million woman-owned businesses, 950,000 of which had paid employees. These figures represented 38 percent of all businesses in the United States and 35 percent of all firms with employees in the United States.[1]

This growth was reflected in the comments of Betsy Myers, then director of the White House Office of Women's Initiatives and Outreach, in a speech in the summer of 1996.

Women's equality is defined by women's economic empowerment. And the ultimate empowerment is through entrepreneurship. Women-owned businesses are the fastest growing force in the US economy, prompting President Clinton to call women business owners "the new face of our economy." When women thrive, their families thrive and the nation thrives.

Inflation-adjusted sales and receipts between 1977 and 1999 for all woman-owned businesses rose by almost 14 percent each year to $3.6 trillion. Woman-owned businesses with employees accounted for 23 percent of sales and receipts for all business in the United States.

Payroll costs for woman-owned businesses with paid employees also rose between 1977 and 1999, growing more than 15 percent each year. Even though the growth rates in these measures were similar, a wide gap developed between sales and receipts and payrolls in firms with paid employees. One of the reasons for the striking growth in woman-owned businesses may be the widening gap between sales and receipts and payroll costs. The gap indicates that substantial profits may have accrued to women business owners. By 1999 about 1 out of every 4 employees in the U.S. worked for a woman-owned firm.

The upsurge in the number of woman-owned businesses, as well as their large volume of sales, receipts, and payrolls, has ensured that women business owners are an economic force that should be considered in policy decisions at every level.

Characteristics of U.S. Women Business Owners

Woman-owned individual proprietorships, partnerships, and subchapter S corporations were in every industrial sector. In 1999 nearly 69 percent of woman-owned firms operated as a service or retail trade; this was 45 percent of all such businesses in the country. While both woman-owned and man-owned firms were most often in the service industries, the second largest group for women was retail trade.[2]

Within retail trade, women business owners were particularly concentrated in apparel and accessory stores, where they owned 54 percent of all firms and accounted for 34 percent of gross receipts. They were also particularly concentrated in miscellaneous retail stores with 53 percent of all firms and 31 percent of gross receipts.

Interestingly, the number of woman-owned construction businesses nearly doubled between 1987 and 1999, while wholesalers increased 87 percent, confirming large growth in the less traditional business sectors for women. Of the receipts generated by woman-owned firms, 64 percent were concentrated in retail trade, services, and wholesale trade. Automotive dealers, gasoline service stations, and miscellaneous retail stores accounted for 54 percent of their retail trade revenue.

According to the data, "traditional" women entrepreneurs before the 1980s tended to be proprietors of small, slow-growing service businesses with low earnings and few assets. "Second-generation" women entrepreneurs started to appear in the 1980s. Many of these women left corporations to start their own firms in nontraditional female business sectors.

Profitablility of Woman-Owned Businesses

Two out of five (40.1 percent) of woman-owned businesses in 1999 were established between 1995 and 1999.

Considering that so many woman-owned firms were very young in 1999, it may not be surprising that two out of five woman-owned businesses had less than $6,200 in receipts in 1999. This complements data indicating that two out of five (42.2 percent) woman-owned businesses had before-tax profits of less than $10,000 in 1992. In addition, 24.6 percent of woman-owned businesses reported before-tax losses. Young firms may need more time and experience before becoming highly successful financial ventures.

It should be noted that 1.3 percent of all woman-owned businesses had receipts of $1 million or more while 1.0 percent of all woman-owned businesses had pretax profits of $100,000 or more.[3]

Home-Based Businesses Among U.S. Women Business Owners

Overall, approximately 40 percent of all woman-owned businesses in 1999 were home-based; 56 percent of individual proprietorships were home-based. While woman-owned and man-owned businesses were almost equally likely to use the residence primarily to do clerical work, woman-owned businesses were substantially more likely to use the home to produce goods and services on the premises than man-owned businesses.[4]

Educational Attainment of Women Business Owners

Over 95 percent of all women business owners possess a high school diploma. In addition, one in five had some college education but no degree. One in five had a bachelor's degree from college.[5]

U.S. WOMEN AND THEIR BUSINESSES

More and more women have found owning their own business a rewarding experience. Not only have women business owners found financial rewards in business ownership, ongoing research for organizations like NAWBO has shown that business ownership opened doors to other rewards, including self-fulfillment. The positive implications associated with owning one's own business suggest that the trend toward greater participation in business ownership by women will continue, despite negative aspects of business ownership such as long hours and high failure rates for young firms.

Angie Kim[6]

Angie Kim, founder of EqualFooting.com, tells an important story about her early years, "When I was in the third grade back in Korea, the teacher asked who wanted to run for class president. I raised my hand, the only girl in the class. The teacher asked me to come to the front, and she spanked my hand with a ruler, saying that girls should know better than to think they can be president of anything." Angie admits to "getting a little satisfaction from that now."

Angie is now president and chief customer officer of EqualFooting.com in Sterling, Virginia—a business-to-business online marketplace that places small manufacturing and construction businesses on equal footing with larger companies. Angie learned about small business after she moved to the United States with her parents from Seoul, Korea, when she was 13. During her teenage years, she learned how small businesses operate by helping her parents build and grow small retail stores. Her family expected her to get a good education and move into a professional career. No one suspected then that she would become an entrepreneur herself before the age of 30 in a groundbreaking business, raising venture capital close to $70 million.

Angie earned a B.A. in philosophy and political science with highest honors from Stanford University. From Stanford, Angie went to Harvard Law School, where she served as an editor of the *Harvard Law Review* and graduated magna cum laude. After law school, she clerked for a chief judge in the U.S. Court of Appeals and then was hired as an attorney by a prestigious law firm in Washington, D.C.

After nearly three years practicing commercial litigation, Angie decided that she preferred building positive business relationships to litigation. She joined McKinsey & Co., a worldwide management consulting agency. Still, she kept thinking about running her own company.

Angie finally launched EqualFooting.com in June 1999 with two former coworkers at McKinsey and seed funding of $1 million from friends, family, and investors. Soon after, they received $7.7 million of venture capital in their first round of funding. Just recently, the company secured an additional $60 million from a top-tier group of leading companies and venture capitalists. EqualFooting.com is using that funding to develop the company's Web site and for marketing.

"We really want to use the power of the Internet to level the playing field for small businesses," she says. "We want to be a one-stop-shop for small businesses, especially in the manufacturing and construction segment." In its first months, the company has grown out of the basement into full offices to house the growing numbers—now 180—of people on its payroll. EqualFooting.com serves small business entrepreneurs who, like Angie, have overcome significant odds to grow their businesses.

Barbara Manzi[7]

Barbara Manzi's ambition was almost crushed when a high school teacher told her "Learn to cook and sew—you're a poor black child and that's the only job you'll ever have." "I vowed," says Barbara, "to prove her wrong." And she did.

Born and raised in a rural area in Massachusetts, Barbara was the third of twelve children. Her family worked "extremely hard" as fishermen and housekeepers just to eke out living. They were poor, but supportive; Barbara felt appreciated at home and it instilled in her a desire to achieve.

Despite the well-intentioned advice of her teacher—who drove her to and from school every day—Barbara did achieve. She mastered cooking and sewing, but she also earned an associate degree in business marketing and business management. She headed for the New York area and built a successful career in retail, eventually becoming a department store manager. Along the way, she also married and had children.

In 1982 Barbara left retail. She used her sales experience and her mathematical ability to get a job with an aerospace supplier, Northern Alloys of Amityville, New York. There she learned all she could about the metal distribution industry and, within a few years, was bringing in $3 million worth of business.

In 1989 Barbara's husband retired from the police force and the family relocated to Florida. There Barbara established a company, and merged with another firm in 1993, but, says Barbara, "I preferred to be in full control of a business." She ended the partnership and started Manzi Metals, Inc., in a spare room in 1995. Her goal: to become one of the foremost metal distributors in the United States.

Once again, she succeeded. Today Manzi Metals distributes aluminum, stainless steel, titanium, and brass and other alloys to aerospace and commercial industries throughout the United States and Canada. The company also supplies raw metals in all shapes and forms. The company is 8(a) and

SDB (small disadvantaged business) certified. Customers include Lockheed Martin, Raytheon, Gulfstream Aerospace, Boeing, and General Motors, as well as shipyards and federal and local government facilities.

Barbara has received many awards, including Lockheed Martin's Woman-Owned Business of the Year in 1995, the Avon Women of Enterprise Award in June 2000, and the Business and Professional Women of Achievement Award.

Barbara says she is lucky to have a family that supports her. Her husband works in the warehouse, shipping and receiving, and quality assurance. Her son is vice president of the company and is in charge of sales and management training. People often ask Barbara how they can start their own businesses and achieve success. "I tell them it takes determination plus hard work," she says.

"My dream is to someday omit the word 'small business' from my credentials and become a large corporation providing jobs and opportunities for the Hernando County area. I believe that within a few years this will become reality," says Barbara.

Nikki Olyai[8]

Nikki Olyai always knew that she wanted her own business. It was her father, a successful businessman in Iran, who was the role model. When she came to the United States at the age of 17—living with a host family in Salem, Oregon, where she attended high school—she knew that she would follow her vision to create and develop her own business.

Undergraduate and graduate degrees in computer science strengthened her resolve. Innovision Technologies started while Nikki Olyai was taking care of her four-year-old son and holding down two other jobs to keep the business rolling. She credits a supportive husband, parents, and family for her ability to continue in spite of obstacles. This year Nikki Olyai was honored by the Women Business Enterprise National Council's "Salute to Women's Business Enterprises" as one of its eleven most successful firms.

In 1999 Innovision Technologies, an IT consulting firm, was ranked number 195 on the *Inc.* 500 list of America's fastest-growing privately held companies. For the third year in a row, her firm was selected as a "Future 50 of Greater Detroit Company."

Emily Harrington[9]

Emily Harrington was born Emily Roxas Sanson in Manila, Philippines, the middle child of nine children. She came to the United States in 1972 as a foreign exchange student, returned to graduate from the Philippines Women's University, and then came back to the United States to work in banking. Not until her father (a successful businessman) asked her to come home and consider starting a business did she think of herself as a possible entrepreneur. "It was his last wish," Harrington says. "He always encouraged me." During the 36-hour trip back to the United States, she decided to quit her job and start a company.

Harrington was motivated to help the many minority women who could not find work. She was convinced that there was a market for hardworking, dedicated minorities and women, and she decided to help them find it. So, in the basement of her home, juggling the care of two small children, she launched the temporary staffing agency, Qualified Resources, Inc. (QRI), that *Inc.* magazine selected as one of "America's Fastest Growing 500 Private Companies" just six years later.

What obstacles has she overcome? "The fact that I'm a minority, that English is my second language, that I'm a small person in stature and a woman—I had all that to overcome plus finding the best child care for two young children while I was trying to launch the business."

Today, Harrington is busy developing a spinoff company—aiming to add technical temporary employees to her roster of employees for hire. As part of her training program for employees and potential employees, she offers English as a second language (ESL), computer skills, and other training before and during placement. More than 200 employees received ESL training through her company. Transportation is an obstacle for some employees. So, to keep them on the job, QRI offers complimentary van services. The result—better attendance and happier clients. QRI serves more than 100 businesses in southern New England, including Brown University, CVS, Fleet Financial Group, and Cumberland Farms. She is also involved in a welfare-to-work project through the Rhode Island Department of Human Services.

Harrington's company is in Cranston and Pawtucket, Rhode Island, and provides temporary and permanent employees for positions in light industry, office administration, management, manufacturing, food services, finance, and technical and professional markets. Annual revenues were nearly $10 million last year; the company placed 3,500 people in jobs and maintains 25 in-house staff. The new division, called QRI Tech PRO will place engineers, production managers, and information technology professionals.

WOMEN-OWNED BUSINESSES OUTSIDE THE UNITED STATES

In the developing world, women are economically active in family enterprises, in their own small businesses, and as employees. The vast majority of this work by women is informal, which gives the women little security or support. Take the stories of the Ugandan business owners:[10]

I started with a few goods because I had little money. I used to pick a few cabbages, but now I buy a whole bag. I buy a whole box of tomatoes. But you have to start small, save slowly, slowly. . . . This season is dead, lost. Things are in pieces. Rains spoiled the harvest. So when you sell, the price is high, beyond what a consumer can afford. . . . We continue to repay our loans, even though we have no money remaining. Work has become more difficult and less rewarding.

> Margaret Namungo, 46, widowed with three children

I eat and drink from my business. I built a house so that I no longer rent. I bought my plot from earnings. I have been able to educate my children. That is very important—an even better achievement than building a house.

> Betty Nakiganda, 48, widowed with eight children,
> sells mangoes

Through my business I have achieved a lot. I managed to construct a house, buy things for it, buy a vehicle, and open two more shops like this one. I believe that there is nothing men can do that we cannot do.

> Teddy Birungi, 36, married with five children,
> wholesales beer, soda, and whiskey

I started what they were calling *magenda* (informal trade) in those days, that is, buying sweets and selling them, making a little profit to add to my salary. Later I baked buns and that was more rewarding. . . . I started looking for a shop. I got a small place in Kisura, but I lived in Nakaserto, so it took me a long time to commute. I had to run the shop after office hours. At 5 p.m., I would collect my children, take them home, give them tea, run through their homework then rush to the shop. Kisura was hard.

> Alice Karaugaba, 50s, separated with four children,
> owns two furniture and soft-goods stores

Clearly, the role of women-owned business is vital to the future and that of their countries. Donald J. Johnston, secretary general of the OECD said in an interview in 1998 on the BBC,

Half of the brainpower on Earth is in the heads of women. Today, the difficulty is to move from the acceptance of equal rights to the reality of equal opportunity. This transition will not be complete until women and men have equal opportunities for occupying positions in power structures throughout the world. This includes not only public law-making and policy-formulating bodies, but also the world of private business. Society as a whole stands to gain by accelerating the process.

Even in the industrialized world, the importance of woman-owned SMEs is beginning to be recognized. Heinrich Kolb, minister of economy in Germany, states

We need to improve the environment for female-owned SMEs, because they are creating scope for more growth employment, broad-space innovation, better skills in the local and global markets. SMEs have to be more forward-looking. In Germany, those women who use government incentives are do-ing as well as men in creating enterprises. Women bring fresh motivation. Women will fit better into the new service society than in the old industrial society. Our countries can no longer do without the expertise, skills and experience of women entrepreneurs.

It is still not easy. In 1992 the Scottish government sought to learn why there were so few female entrepreneurs in the country and to help close the gap between Scotland and the rest of the United King-dom in terms of the number of new woman-led firms created.

Although the number of self-employed women in Scotland doubled over the period of 1980–90 only 5 percent of Scotland's working women were self-employed (or 56,000 out of a female working pop-ulation of just over one million). This is around half the proportion of the rest of Great Britain, and far less than elsewhere. For instance, 40 percent of Germany's new firms were set up by women, and in the United States in 1993 the figure was 70 percent.[11]

The key problem, according to research conducted by the Scottish Enterprise, is converting widespread interest in entrepreneurship into actual businesses. In other words, persuading more women to convert interest into action. This gap between those expressing an interest and those taking action to establish businesses is chiefly to do with a lack of self-confidence and an absence of knowledge of the process of business creation.

Growth was also found to be more stymied in woman-owned busi-nesses, either by choice (because of the need to combine family com-mitments and work) or because resistance to female entrepreneurship is more common among males in Scotland than elsewhere (resulting in a lack of support from family or financially).

Because of this, the availability of support, such as good child care, is an important prerequisite for many would-be women entrepreneurs. In Glasgow, where only 2.5 percent of working women are self-employed, a women's enterprise network has been formed to offer women advice on setting up their own businesses and overcoming some of the obstacles women face. Similar networks and initiatives have been set up throughout the country.

According to the assistant director of Glasgow Opportunities Enterprise Trust, one of the biggest problems women face is overcoming the macho culture of the west of Scotland. She said women also had to view self-employment as a positive option rather than a last resort in the face of unemployment.[12] The following cultural attitudes were found to be particularly strong in Scotland:

• Negative attitudes to enterpreneurship. People surveyed in Scotland had much less positive views of how much entrepreneurs contribute to society than people elsewhere.

• The term *entrepreneur* itself suggested negative images of ruthless tycoons.

• Women felt a need to accommodate male-dominated norms in their approach to business in order to accommodate a possible negative reaction from men.

Sandra Arnold-Griffin, an established entrepreneur in the United States who moved to Scotland, exemplifies the situation of Scottish women: "I've changed my style and approach since coming to Scotland. In the States I would be much more up-front and readily taking charge. But here I knew it could cause me problems. I tend to play things down more, too."[13]

The lack of spouse and family support women entrepreneurs receive is also a factor. The research revealed that Scottish males have particularly negative attitudes about women seeking to achieve entrepreneurial success, contributing to the low participation of women in many business startup courses and services and the high dropout rate of women from such programs.

An atmosphere of encouragement and enthusiasm toward woman-owned businesses is growing, with increasing initiatives on building business skills and networking with other women. A new business group in Edinburgh is encouraging would-be women entrepreneurs to "set up shop." Sheena Doneghan, the group's founder, realized there was a need to fill the gap between support groups for businesswomen who have already made it and the general business startup groups for both men and women.

Last year Doneghan returned to Edinburgh to start her own consultancy, Sheena Doneghan Associates, after a successful retail marketing career in London.

I had to start making contacts from scratch and found there were plenty of groups and organizations to join. But they were more geared toward those who were already established and successful, and not necessarily appropriate to new businesswomen. I thought, "Where do women go who do not have a lot of faith in themselves, who want to set up on their own, but aren't sure how to go about it?" Women just starting up on their own are sometimes intimidated by business groups. I've also heard them say that men can hijack meetings. I felt there were no courses or groups available to help women think about self employment from a belief perspective, with role models who could tell them I did it and it was frightening—but I did it.[14]

Doneghan has led several Women in Business seminars in Edinburgh. These seminars focus on women's self-awareness, exploring whether self-employment is a suitable option for the individual, and helping women identify the skills they already have and how they could be transferred to a business setting. "It's not easy to be self-employed," admits Doneghan, "So it's important to look at all the considerations and decide whether this type of lifestyle will suit your life."

Irene Pivetti, former president of the Parliament of Italy, agrees when she says, "Spreading entrepreneurship in general, and women's entrepreneurship in particular, has always relied on local culture and local social capital. Where entrepreneurship thrives, it is because local values and political powers implement a policy conducive to an enhanced role for women and entrepreneurship in general."[15]

Once the recognition of the need to empower women through the support of female entrepreneurship is completed, it becomes necessary to understand the primary economic, social, and personal motivations for women to start businesses. The next three chapters will explore them.

NOTES

1. The data for this analysis came from the economic census *Economic Census Women-Owned Businesses*, and *Economic Census Characteristics of Business Owners* for 1999 and in selected prior years. The Bureau of the Census conducts an economic census every five years, covering years ending in 4 and 9. Special programs cover enterprise statistics and minority- and woman-owned businesses.

2. According to records from the Internal Revenue Service, www.irs.gov.

3. Ibid.

4. According to records from the United States Commerce Department.

5. Ibid.

6. This story appeared on the web site for the U.S. Small Business Administration's Women's Online Center, www.sba.gov.

7. Ibid.

8. Ibid.

9. Ibid.

10. From interviews with Andrew R. Thomas, March 2000.

11. Brenda L. Hudson, "Women's Entrepreneurship in Scotland," *Advancing Women Network*, AdvancingWomen.com

12. Ibid.

13. Ibid.

14. Ibid.

15. European Database, "Women in Decision-Making," www.db-decision .de, August 2001.

5

Economic Motivations for Female Entrepreneurs

The sea hath bounds, but deep desire hath none.
William Shakespeare

Motivation is a close cousin to strife. The entrepreneurial spirit is commonly about overcoming obstacles. Women's stories are especially intriguing because the obstacles can be many and profound. Women entrepreneurs often lack capital, procurement opportunities, training, mentors, and respect. What they don't lack is will.

Social expectations of women's role and family responsibilities usually mean that women assume a greater responsibility for household, child care, and dependent care, which can be a burden for women trying to manage and balance these responsibilities while trying to grow their businesses. In some countries, women are less welcome in social networks (for instance, going out after work for cocktails), which excludes them from opportunities, which limits their access to often critical information. As a result, social structures and the way that women socialize influence the human and social capital endowments with which they start their businesses.

Despite these and countless other barriers, women are starting businesses worldwide in record numbers. They are improving their lives, those of their families, and the conditions of their communities. Recognizing their primary motivations for starting businesses allows us to better understand the global rise of female entrepreneurs and how to better deliver effective programs in support of woman-owned businesses.

Clearly, no single factor motivates a woman to build her own company. Her reasons depend upon several personal and external circumstances, both positive and negative. These chapters will explore women's primary and most deep-seated motivations for starting and running their own businesses: economic, social, and personal.

THE DIFFICULTY OF OBTAINING DATA TO DESIGN POLICY

Good information is essential for the design of sound, appropriate policies. It is not easy to determine the number of women entrepreneurs from official statistics in either developed or developing countries. The figures are often incomplete or based on samples. In many countries, there is no clear definition of what constitutes a female enterprise. For example, firms are sometimes classified according to their turnover, number of employees, or legal status. Statistics on women are problematic, since most surveys do not take gender into account.

This situation is partly due to historical factors or civil liberties that prohibit the collection and publication of certain information by national statistical systems. Detailed statistics on income and wealth are therefore particularly difficult to obtain from some countries. Organizing international data poses the additional problems of access and lack of comparability.

Moreover, in spite of recent improvements, women business owners have not received the attention they deserve from national and local authorities, educational institutions or from the world of business and finance. Because obtaining needed information is difficult, those who support female entrepreneurs must look elsewhere for guidance in designing polices. Understanding the motivations provides us with this guidance.

ECONOMIC MOTIVATIONS

One of the most universal motivations for women starting businesses is the need to generate income. If women had the same opportunities to make money in jobs as men, the energy behind this motivation would be much less. In all countries women are at an economic disadvantage compared to men, even in industrialized countries. Societal norms still discount women as the primary bread-winners in the family.

With the increase in divorce and women heading single-parent households, in many cases they are the primary breadwinners. This is especially the case in the developing world, where it is common for one man to father numerous children without providing economic support to any of the offspring. The changing economy is also creating an economic need for women. The globalization of the world's economy and the downsizing of larger companies are eliminating jobs that are traditionally female. The beauty of this story though, is that women are taking their economic future into their own hands by starting their own enterprises. By running their own businesses, they have a direct relationship between how hard they work and how much money they earn. While they may in some cases make less money initially by choosing to own a business, they know in the long run they have more security and potential for earnings when they own the business.

ECONOMIC MOTIVATIONS IN DEVELOPED COUNTRIES

In many developed countries, the changing nature of government programs coupled with the lack of opportunity for entry-level work has led many women to view entrepreneurship as the best way out of the permanent cycle of poverty. As a result, many women look at their own business as the best way to achieve those things the system failed to provide.

After realizing dependence on government programs was doing nothing to improve their self-esteem, many women have tried to enter the workplace. Although the economies of the United States and Western Europe have created millions of new jobs in recent years, they found that entry-level positions often do not pay enough to provide the basic necessities. As a result, many women rejected government assistance, started a new job, and, at the same time, launched a new business. The combination of the salary and benefits received from their job and the extra income from their own business provides many with enough resources to sustain themselves and their families for the long term.

E. Jeanne Tyson[1]

E. Jeanne Tyson's story is typical of that of many women whose primary motivation for starting her business was economic. In 1994 Tyson decided that living on public assistance was doing nothing for her and her two young daughters. As part of a federally funded program, Tyson enrolled in the local community college where, after two years, she graduated with her associate degree in business.

Immediately upon graduation, Tyson began working for a local health-care provider in their billing office. Although the job was good one, it didn't pay enough to allow her to move out of public housing. Desperately wanting her daughters to attend a better school system, Tyson soon realized she would need to do something else to augment her salary.

While working for the health-care provider, Tyson soon discovered that there was a tremendous need in the community for home-based care that was completely neglected by the existing firms. She opened Royalty Home Health Care Services to meet that need in October 1994. Short on financing but long on desire, Tyson spent her days off and lunch breaks visiting banks, credit unions, and any other lending institution that would listen to her. As so often happens, everybody listened but, at the end, nobody gave her a loan. Dejected and seemingly out of options, she got a call out of the blue from a friend who said that Enterprise Development Corporation had just established a microloan program and was looking for candidates. After a three-hour presentation in front of local managers, Tyson was granted a $3,250 loan. Her collateral was three used desks, three used chairs, a filing cabinet, a typewriter, three new telephones, a 1981 Mercury, and her niece's 1982 Toyota.

Having secured the critical money to get started, Tyson then needed to find some customers. With the help of family and friends, Royalty Health Care Services' flyers were posted in every laundry, grocery store, service station, church lobby, and public gathering place in the area. Tyson also personally visited every hospital, nursing home, and social service agency in the area to introduce her new company to them. Not content to stop there, she spoke to area ladies clubs that served senior women. She personally handed out thousands of flyers and never turned down a chance to be at a health fair or gathering. She did all this while working a full-time job and raising two young daughters! After a couple of months, the phones started ringing.

In the early days, Royalty boasted a staff of one nurse, two aides, and one office person (Tyson). Like her employees, Tyson struggled with child-care issues as well as the burden of finding and keeping reliable transportation. She met child-care challenges by bringing her daughters to work or forwarding the office phone to her home. The car presented greater problems. She readily admits that intervention from a higher power is all that kept her from having to walk home on more than one cold winter night.

The early achievements were overshadowed by the stark realities of how cash flow was impeded by delayed reimbursements. On more than one occasion, there was insufficient money to meet the payroll. Each time she called her employees together to deliver the bad news. And each time, her employees restated their commitment to her and said they were confident she would pay them and they could wait for their paychecks. By 1995 Jeanne Tyson welfare mom had become Jeanne Tyson small-business owner: $40,000 in debt with a marathon work schedule.

Undaunted, she fought and battled every step along the way to make Royalty a household name in the community. Countless times she could have given up and taken the path of least resistance, but Jeanne, like millions of female entrepreneurs around the world, never once lost sight of her goal. She, like them, responded to every setback with more determination. "I've survived everything so far," she'd say each time. "I'm not giving up now." She adds that Royalty Health Care Services is her children's legacy.

Today, Royalty Health Care Services is housed in its own office complex with a fifty-person staff and an impressive bottom line. Tyson is driving a new van and has just returned with her daughters from their first-ever vacation—to Disney World.

Phyllis Cano[2]

As a child, Phyllis Cano often went to Woolworth's on 16th Street to watch the cake decorator demonstrate her skill. "She fascinated me. I'd say, 'That's what I want to be when I grow up.' "

Married at 16 and divorced at 19, Cano was on welfare for six years because she had two children to support. During that time, she went to Emily Griffith Opportunity School in Denver and earned a certificate in cake decorating. She also studied psychology and mechanical drafting and worked drawing maps. When that job ended, Cano decided to pursue her first love: cakes.

Cano was hired by a Denver custom-cake company, but after a year she had differences with the owner and left. "By working with her I got to see how to run a business," Cano says.

Having found her passion, Phyllis now needed to find the capital to start her own business. With support from the Mi Casa Resource Center for Women, she obtained a $5,000 loan from the Greater Local Development Corporation. In business since 1997, she now employs five and includes Baby Doe's, Brittany Hill, Weberg's, Brewski's, and Arapahoe Junction in her major accounts.

Growing her business slowly but surely, Phyllis is confident she will succeed, despite the obstacles facing her as a single mother and former welfare recipient.

Linda Torres-Winters[3]

The daughter of migrant workers, Linda Torres-Winters grew up picking tomatoes in the Midwest. "We lived in one big room, side by side—seven children," says Linda. She picked her first tomatoes at the age of 6. Then, when she was 16, her father was disabled in a work accident. Linda left school and took on a second job to help support her family.

What she couldn't know then was that it was tomatoes—stirred together with determination and seasoned with inspiration—that would lead to entrepreneurial success. Early on, the drive was there. "I always wanted to do something for my family and be somebody," she says.

At the age of 17, Linda earned her high school equivalency certificate. She then became the first person in her family to attend college, enrolling in the University of Wisconsin at Milwaukee. While there, she worked with the high school equivalency program, helping others earn their certificates.

Linda married and had two children, all the while fostering an entrepreneurial dream. Eventually, she decided to make her dream come true—and she wanted to do it by developing something that would honor her Hispanic heritage. That's where the tomatoes come in.

"I can remember my mother making the best salsa," Linda says. Starting with that inspiration, she created a salsa mix with a twist: it's dry, based on the dehydrated spices and vegetables Linda used on family camping trips. You just add fresh or canned tomatoes for "homemade" salsa, any time, anywhere. What's more, you can have it either hot or mild.

A year later, Linda signed a contract with Safeway—and Lindita's took off. The company's products are now available in more than 500 stores in eight states.

ECONOMIC MOTIVATIONS IN COUNTRIES IN TRANSITION

In some countries, unemployment and the lack of other economic options is the major factor in why women go into business for themselves. This is particularly true in countries that are undergoing transition from a planned, state-run economy to a more open one. Women in the transition economies are increasingly turning to entrepreneurship.

Statistical data broken down by gender are scarce in the transition economies, but evidence there suggests that women, who are particularly affected by the privatization of state-owned industries and the structural unemployment resulting from the transition to market economies, are increasingly turning to entrepreneurship.

Before the fall of the Berlin Wall, 94 percent of women in the former German Democratic Republic worked. Today, the 20 percent unemployment rate in eastern Germany has touched off a surge in female entrepreneurship: 150,000 new female-run companies have been launched since 1990.[4]

Before its transition from a planned economy, very many women participated in the labor force in Hungary. Since the transition, the number of jobs dropped and the economically inactive population rose.

The unemployment rate among women increased from 0.4 percent in 1990 to 10.0 percent in 1995; in numbers, this was an increase from 10,000 to 217,000. In 1985, 70.1 percent of women aged 15 to 64 worked; that percentage decreased to 60.0 by 1992.

Working women have changed their views of women's employment since the transition. In 1986, 81 percent of employed women said women should engage in paid work. In 1995 only 66 percent of employed women believed the same.

However, women, once unemployed, spend more time unemployed than men and have more difficulty finding jobs than men. Other indicators of the difference between men's and women's employment are that 52 percent of women work for entirely state-owned enterprises (33 percent of men do) and that 9 percent of women work less than 36 hours per week compared to 3.7 percent of men. In similar jobs, women's salaries lag 10.5 percent behind men's. A result of the difference in wages is lower benefits (unemployment, sickness, and pensions are all based on earnings).

As a result of the transition from a planned economy to a free market, women in Hungary make up 41.1 percent of all entrepreneurs in enterprises established after 1990, an increase from 29.3 percent prior to 1990. Recent studies suggest Hungarian women entrepreneurs have higher educational achievement than the average woman worker. Nearly 83 percent of the women entrepreneurs work full-time. Almost 50 percent of all Hungarian woman-owned SMEs were owned by women between the ages of 40 and 54. And 72 percent of women entrepreneurs are married.[5]

ECONOMIC MOTIVATIONS IN THE
DEVELOPING WORLD

Although some women do undoubtedly succeed in becoming quite successful entrepreneurs, most poor women are likely to face serious problems. In some countries, particularly in Africa, Latin America, and Asia, there are well-established traditions of female entrepreneurship and large-scale trading.

Even in societies where women are in strict seclusion, they frequently engage in business activities from the home and have in some cases built up substantial enterprises. Women frequently become quite substantial entrepreneurs in particular sectors where female labor predominates, and women may in fact dominate these industries.

Women in the developing world are overwhelmingly clustered in a narrow range of low-investment, low-profit activities for the local market. In many of these industries, there are likely to be definite limits on the ability of small-scale independent women producers to increase their incomes because of intense competition from capital-intensive or large-scale production.

Despite their diversity, gender inequalities compound those of class to make small-scale entrepreneurship even more difficult for poor women than for poor men.

As in the rest of the world, the economic motivation for starting a business is prevalent in the developing world. Many women are being pushed into whatever market economic activity they can take up. Decreasing opportunities for men to earn a family wage and the increasing disruption of family ties with economic development have made many women less able to depend on customary forms of male support. In many cases male expectations that women will contribute to the family income pool have increased.

Women often do business in the informal sector as a desperate effort when there are few alternatives, rather than as a conscious choice. In handicraft industries in West Bengal and the South Indian silk-reeling industry, for example, women were very interested in the possibility of entrepreneurship as an improvement on the conventional income-generation programs available to them.

The economic motivation for women to start businesses has grown out of financial conditions that have forced women to find alternative methods for generating income. In many countries, women have less economic clout than men do. Even in the United States, we still hear stories of a man being paid a higher salary than a woman for the same job.

Women who have had the good fortune to live in countries with capitalist economies have been blessed with an environment that allows them to take fate into their own hands in the form of business ownership. Those who have not been so fortunate have often still found ways to create their own enterprises outside the formal business world.

The growth in women entrepreneurs from economic motivation demonstrates the resiliency and steadfastness of women. Women entrepreneurs worldwide have demonstrated their ability to take control of their economic future, by choosing the risky and often difficult option of entrepreneurship.

NOTES

1. From interview with authors, November 1999.

2. This story appeared on the web site for the U.S. Small Business Administration's Women's Online Center, www.sba.gov.

3. Ibid.

4. Liba Pauykert, "Economic Transition and Women's Employment", Paper for Employment Department, International Labor Office, 1995, Geneva.

5. Ibid.

6

Social Motivations for Female Entrepreneurs

Never doubt the fact that a few dedicated people can change the world.

Margaret Meade

Before the Industrial Revolution, families generally lived and worked in the same place. The family farm created work for men and women alike. Each played a role in the family and they operated as a unit. Families were physically close, and so they had a built-in support mechanism in the case of sick children, an aging parent, or family crises. A family who owned a retail store would often employ the mother and her children, who would help around the store when they weren't in school. In today's modern society, the family and taking care of the family have become separated from the role of breadwinner. Earning a living usually requires leaving the home and often the community to work for long hours in an environment completed separated from home and family.

THE IMPORTANCE OF FAMILY

Men and women both are finding that they crave a blending of their family and work life rather than complete separation. The schedule that is imposed on working mothers makes it nearly impossible to respond to the personal needs of a family. By starting their own businesses, women are creating an environment where they are in control of where they work, how they work, and when they work. Although they often work as many hours or more than they did when employed, they are more in control of their time and they can work their business around the needs of their families instead of the other way around.

Janice DiMichele[1]

As a product manager at General Electric (GE), Janice DiMichele had achieved a great deal of success in one of America's finest companies by the time she had reached her early 30s. The good salary, complete benefits, and stock options were very attractive to Janice and her husband. Nevertheless, when Janice had her first baby, everything changed. As a new mother, Janice decided it was much more important for her to be with her new baby than to work. It was a surprise to everyone when Janice announced that she was leaving General Electric after fourteen years of dedicated service.

Janice's bosses at GE were shocked and asked if there was any way that they could persuade her to stay on. The only solution, Janice said, was to allow her the flexibility to be with her new baby and, at the same time, effectively do her job. After much deliberation, GE offered Janice a part-time position in the same department, doing pretty much the same job as before. Over the next three years, Janice and her husband had two more children while she continued in her part-time role. Being able to work and still spend time with her children gave Janice a tremendous sense of fulfillment. Then the human resources department and upper management decided that Janice could no longer work in her "special" part-time role. She would have to decide between a full-time position or none at all.

Having seen firsthand that it was possible to strike the difficult balance between work and family, Janice decided to start her own business. Like many women, Janice's overriding motivation was social—to build a business around the time with her family—not the time with her family around the business. As a result, Peabody's Toys That Teach, Inc. was born. From the renovated basement and garage of her home, Janice's company produces and distributes Fact Packs™, Post-Ables™, and Kard Kits™. The interactive card and pencil sets are designed to give kids something creative to do that promotes learning and the use of their imagination. Janice's company sells and distributes her products to restaurant chains like Big Boy and Alabama Bar and Grille and tourist destinations like Sea World, Smithsonian Institution, the U.S. Capitol, and the Henry Ford Museum.

As business volume demands it, Janice will hire between six and eight individuals to help her prepare the orders. It is not surprising that all Janice's employees are moms who have decided to stay home and work part-time in order to achieve the important balance between work and family.

Luisa Hechavarrias[2]

A Denver resident, Luisa Hechavarrias, 36, opened Friendly Auto Glass in March 1994 with the help of a $2,000 microloan from the Colorado National Bank Community Enterprise Lending Initiative (CELI) program. She repaid the loan, received an additional $5,000 loan, employs a full-time worker, and doubled sales from her first year in business.

"It's lucrative," says Hechavarrias. "I can see the growth. If I keep at it, I'll eventually be able to save for the future and for my children."

Hechavarrias manages the firm from her house on Elati Street, just two blocks from the Mi Casa Business Center for Women in Denver. This allows her to cut costs and keep tabs on her three children, ages 10, 5 and 4. While some of her clients live in the neighborhood, she targets suburban Aurora, Colorado, in her marketing plan. A Yellow Pages® ad reads, "Se Habla Español. Friendly Auto Glass. 10% Discount If You Mention This Ad." The ad generates calls seven days a week. "We get a lot of calls on the weekend," Hechavarrias says. "People get really nervous about their cars and they want it taken care of as soon as possible."

Melissa Morris[3]

For twelve years, Melissa Morris worked in public relations and marketing for a major media corporation, a job that meant dealing with a 9 to 5 office grind that left her little time to spend with her two children. When she found herself a casualty of corporate downsizing, Melissa decided she would rather trust her future to herself than to somebody else.

"For the first four years of my children's life, I felt as though I was missing something while working outside the home. Then one day I found myself without a job or office and realized I would be happier working from home and near my children," explains Melissa.

Having little luck finding a job that met her needs, Melissa decided to take a gamble and bet on herself as a boss and a business owner. Using her considerable public relations and marketing experience, Beth decided to start a business helping moms and other "wannabe" entrepreneurs create and build their own businesses. Dubbing her consulting business SMART-MOMS, Inc., Melissa set to work empowering and educating moms in how to create, build, and sustain their own entrepreneurial businesses. Naming her business was a blend of serendipity and subliminal common sense.

"It's funny how I came up with the name for my business," explains Melissa. "I remember thinking over and over how moms are some of the smartest people I know and how great it would be to help them make their dreams a reality.

"Then one night, I just woke up out of a dead sleep, with two words on my mind—'Smart Moms.' I ran to my computer, did a quick domain name search, and finding the name unclaimed, registered it and, voila! My business was born!"

Drawing from years of experience helping her employers build and market their businesses and products, Melissa decided to coach and mentor entrepreneurs as a consultant and teacher to help them reach their dreams.

"I work very closely with my clients," says Melissa. "Exploring business options, helping them write their business plan, figuring out tax issues . . . finding customers, I am there every step of the way coaching and guiding them toward their goals."

Since Melissa's business extends itself to virtually every state in America, she has developed innovative uses of technology to communicate and coach her clients.

"I use my computer and telephone extensively in my business. Not only do I advise my clients using e-mail, but I also teach a marketing/advertising class using teleconferencing," explains Melissa. "I teach these classes late at night to meet the needs of my clients and offer them a low-cost way of learning. It's been very effective."

Forging her own niche opportunity, Melissa combined her business savvy with a lot of moxie. "After twelve years of working in the public relations, marketing and advertising business, I knew exactly what I needed to succeed. If you have the desire, nothing will stop you."

With a lot of effort and ingenuity, Melissa was able to build her own Web site and taught herself enough to host it herself. "I wanted to have control over how my Web site was set up, so I'd work on it in the wee hours of the morning while everybody was asleep to get it up and running. I'm very proud of how it's all turned out."

Melissa began her marketing efforts by "walking her talk"—more specifically, she designed tee and sweat shirts with her logo, "I'm a Smart Mom" emblazened across it. People seeing her out and about would ask her what her shirt meant, effectively opening the door to discussion and ultimately snagging customers.

"I really preach and practice the 'three foot rule,' " explains Melissa. "Anybody who comes within three feet of me is going to get an earful about my business. Word of mouth is an extremely effective way of finding customers and it costs you nothing!"

After a year, Melissa expanded her marketing efforts to include sending out press releases and writing articles for various parenting publications. Soon, word of her business garnered her an infomercial gig, a feature in *Metro Parent* magazine, and a profile on Fox News as a successful entrepreneur.

"The publicity has been terrific," beams Melissa. "It's been a lot of hard work, but it's really paying off."

With all the success Melissa has enjoyed, her greatest enjoyment has come from knowing she has helped other moms, like herself, realize their dreams and achieve success. "I'm very proud of what I have been able to accomplish and give back to moms around the country," smiles Melissa. "I love what I do—I have the best of all worlds."

Kathy Benson and Sue Lynd[4]

Kathy Benson and Sue Lynd launched their data-collection business more than nine years ago with a vision in mind: to create a flexible workplace for women. Office Remedies, Inc. (ORI), was designed to allow women the opportunity to work from their homes and to work hours that fit their schedules. Kathy and Sue integrated their vision into their corporate mission statement, business plan, and marketing materials.

In nine years, ORI has grown from a home-based data-entry company to a leader in the data-collection arena, providing high-tech, full-service data entry, scanning, and imaging. Staff has grown from several part-time employees to four full-time, and up to fifty part-time, employees. The company has contracts with Fortune 500 companies and large enterprises in the metropolitan Washington, D.C., area.

ORI offers the following services: keypunch entry of names, addresses, and surveys; survey development; data analysis; database design and maintenance; scanning and imaging; optical character recognition (OCR) editing and cleanup; and coding and indexing.

The company has competed based on its ability to maintain a high level of accuracy and deliver quality service in a timely manner, as well as giving personalized attention to each project.

Margaret McClain-McEntire[5]

When Margaret McClain-McEntire started her "little" business in her garage, she never dreamed that ten years later she would have 410 stores with revenues over $40 million—one of the fastest-growing franchises in the United States.

It was a simple idea that worked—offering delicious chocolates and candies in bright, colorful arrangements as an alternative to sending flowers. "I just knew that everyone liked flowers and everyone likes to eat candy— so how could we combine the two?" Margaret explains that florists had been working for years trying to create such a mix, but no one succeeded, until she "stumbled on it." "I had no preconceived ideas," says Margaret. She credits a friend with an engineering background and another in the decorating business with helping to develop the perfect technique.

The first Candy Bouquet store opened in Houston in 1989 with a partner running it. "People were tearing down the paper around the store before we even opened, asking where they could get the candy bouquets. I knew we had a winner!"

One year after the business opened, with no advance notice, Margaret's partner announced that she was closing the store and moving away. Margaret's life savings were invested in the business, but she was determined to start over. With her husband's support, she moved the business to Little Rock, Arkansas. Then, in 1992, her husband's company collapsed; he moved his business into their home and Margaret took over managing the books. She also was home-schooling two of their three children and running a household; only in her "spare" time could she go to the garage to make candy bouquets.

Although the bouquets looked good, not enough people in Little Rock knew about her product. To promote her wares, Margaret began giving away bouquets in high-traffic locations such as banks, popular restaurants, and cleaners. As a result, people started calling, some to place orders and others to learn how to make the bouquets. That's how the Candy Bouquet franchise began.

The company's growth pattern has been "strong and steady . . . not greedy." Margaret's own children are growing up, and so she has more time for the business, but also more responsibility as president of a major operation, including franchise grooming and training. She also develops new variations of the business, such as providing jobs for disabled people and launching charity ventures.

These women's stories reflect the sentiment of millions of entrepreneurs who are starting businesses because of their desire to find balance between work and home. Clearly, changes in society, which have put more pressure on many women to "have it all," have actually been a driving force behind the growth of female entrepreneurs—especially in developed countries.

Frustrated by their need to work, but unwilling to accept the terms of employment, many women have struck out on their own. Added to this frustration is the dynamic of the huge segment of the baby boomer population that is becoming sandwiched between the raising of children and the caring of aging parents. The women who find themselves in this position, many of whom have fought their way into executive positions, find a keen desire for the flexibility and control that entrepreneurship provides.

NOTES

1. Interview with authors, November 1999.
2. This story appeared on the Web site for the U.S. Small Business Administration's Women's Online Center, www.sba.gov.
3. Ibid.
4. Ibid.
5. Ibid.

7

Personal Motivations for Female Entrepreneurs

There is no act, large or small, fine or mean, which springs from any motive but the one—the necessity of appeasing and contenting one's own spirit.

Mark Twain

The third and most interesting of the motivators for women entrepreneurs is the need to be personally fulfilled. Even in the developing world where the primary motivation is economic, the motivation for self-fulfillment is very strong. Women who have struggled with the welfare system and tried desperately to support their families discover a newfound sense of accomplishment in supporting themselves.

Many female entrepreneurs start their businesses because of a social or spiritual need they identify in their lives. Others have a vision of a better way to build a mousetrap. These women share the common motivation of self-fulfillment and the desire to be in control of their destiny. Often self-fulfillment will keep a women entrepreneur in business even when she would gain more economic benefit working for someone else.

The desire for self-fulfillment is particularly strong for women, since many societies give women little respect for their accomplishments and abilities and therefore crave an opportunity to create their own self-respect.

Looking at the rewards of entrepreneurship, most women business owners seem to agree that the greatest rewards of entrepreneurship come from within—strongly related to the empowerment derived from being in charge of one's own fate. Issues related to gaining control and independence are the greatest rewards of business ownership:

- Having control over one's own destiny
- Gaining independence and freedom
- Achieving growth and personal balance
- Feeling pride and self-esteem

The rewards of business ownership for women also include the satisfaction of building and growing a business, as well as employing people and helping them achieve their full potential.

Noreen Roman[1]

Noreen Roman reflects the importance of personal motivations as she strives to make her business succeed. Her firm, Birth and Beyond, Inc., offers postpartum *doula* services and professional support for new mothers. Trained originally as a medical technologist and also the holder of an MBA, Noreen says the primary motivation for starting her business was to help society return to the traditional model of women helping women.

Doula is a Greek word that translates as "woman servant." In many developing countries, *Doula*s are women designated by the community to help new mothers deal with the stress and strain of postpartum issues. Although most cultures throughout history have recognized the need to attend to the mother after their delivery, today's fast-paced lifestyle in the United States does not. Moreover, our society tends to minimize the importance of postpartum needs. Instead, women are expected to "bounce back" and "be back to normal" within a couple of days. As any new mom will tell you, it sounds good in theory but doesn't work that way in reality.

Noreen's company and other *doula* service firms like hers are dedicated to providing women of all backgrounds the care all new mothers need. Sibling care, breast and bottle feeding help, meal preparation, grocery shopping, and light housekeeping are some of its services. Birth and Beyond, Inc., is dedicated to alleviating the natural anxiety that follows childbirth. When talking to Noreen and others like her, one is struck by the unwavering commitment these women have to giving of themselves and to fulfilling their personal ambition of creating a better world. Their businesses are merely manifestations of this commitment.

FED UP WITH THE "GLASS CEILING"

A significant number of women business owners take the risky step of starting businesses because they run into a "glass ceiling" or feel unchallenged in their work.

According to a study of female entrepreneurs conducted by the National Foundation for Women Business Owners and the Committee of 200, 16 percent of the women respondents cited a "glass ceiling"—an invisible barrier to advancement—as a significant motivation for becoming entrepreneurs. It is interesting that 22 percent of men business owners cited a "glass ceiling" as a reason for starting their own company, a slightly higher percentage than women. But women reported much stronger barriers. A third of women owners said that they had strongly experienced not being taken seriously by their employers, compared with only 18 percent of men.[2]

Women coming from the corporate world are particularly frustrated, with many saying their employers didn't take them seriously or value them, the study reported. Almost 60 percent of women who had come from corporations said nothing would induce them to return, including more money or flexibility. The appearance of a large number of female entrepreneurs in the economy is something new. Until recently, when women went to work they entered organizations. So many, in fact, that by the 1980s, workforce demographics had been irrevocably altered.

In various degrees, most companies accommodated to the change. Today, nearly all are aware that, according to demographic projections, in the coming decades companies will not be able to prosper or perhaps even survive without recruiting and promoting women managers.

Changing corporate cultures has been difficult. While it is clear that women are achieving greater upward mobility, breaking into the highest ranks is extremely rare. Top management and the corporate boards of Fortune 500 companies remain predominately male. According to the New York nonprofit women's research group Catalyst, today women constitute only 2 percent of corporate America's top earners. Few sit on the boards of directors of the largest corporations.

Faced with limited advancement opportunities and weary of being sidetracked, a number of talented and capable women grew disillusioned with corporate life and politics and left. The frustration became so widespread and noticeable that when Ann Morrison, Randall White, and Ellen Van Velsor titled their 1977 book *Breaking the Glass*

Ceiling, the phrase stuck. Discrimination also played a role in corporate exits. One 1990 study by the group "9 to 5" reported that 46 percent of the female professionals surveyed reported that they experienced discrimination at work.

Although many aspects of business ownership have no gender boundaries, certain challenges are common to female entrepreneurs. The biggest reward is the empowerment that comes with gaining control over your destiny. The most significant challenge many women entrepreneurs apparently face is being taken seriously, which includes the following elements:

• Proving their capability and credibility
• Competing and succeeding in a male-dominated environment
• Overcoming sexism, discrimination, and stereotypes

For a large majority of women entrepreneurs, owning and operating a business becomes an important part of their careers. Some business owners began their entrepreneurial careers early, capitalizing on a talent or skill, and worked in their own businesses from then on. For others, establishment of a firm came after a usually lengthy period of organizational life and was built on the bedrock of accumulated business skills. Still others tracked back and forth between working for others and owning and operating businesses of their own.

These women became good managers, learned to plan well, to readily identify the key elements that related to operations under their control, and to adapt quickly. As managers, they did not operate through traditional organizational hierarchies in authoritarian fashion but tended to prefer to work through networks and teams.

Hard work, busy lives, and sacrifices were the norm. While success seldom came easily, the road to it usually began with spotting an opportunity. Many of these women founded their businesses in search of new challenges, to be in charge, and to accomplish something.

Those who left their previous organizational environments, mostly large companies, did so for a variety of reasons. Some saw business possibilities where the managers in their corporate environments did not and left to pursue them.

Others sought to escape stifling workplaces, looked for new horizons in fields where they had gained experience, calculated a new path, and then left. Some were influenced in their decisions by the special effects that gender still confers: work environments hostile to women, lingering discrimination, inequitable compensation, and differential treatment.

Several were caught in mergers, downsizing, or other changes and had to reorder their lives in a hurry. Some exhibited great creativity in jumping from one field to another entirely unrelated to what they had been doing.

Nearly all women entrepreneurs have an important plot line in common. At a critical time in her career, someone with whom she had connected offered encouragement, pointed out an opportunity, provided financial backing, or in some other important way lent a hand. The commonality of such incidents cannot be dismissed as good luck, unless in the sense of the old saying that chance favors the well prepared.

Career planning for these women in the new work environment requires rethinking old assumptions. Until recently, people tended to think of the world of work in distinct categories. Most people worked either in someone else's business or in their own. The distinction between being an employee and being an entrepreneur was clear.

For those who worked in large organizations, there was a well-understood implied contract that if you did your work well you would remain employed and be rewarded because the company was a near permanent fixture in the landscape.

The rapid changes in the economy in the past two decades have called this contract into question. People learned that the meaning of the word *employment* has irrevocably changed. While a pattern still remains, one simply cannot depend on the traditional arrangements of lifetime jobs and corporate or professional advancement.

What count now are portable skills and knowledge, meaningful work, on-the-job learning, and contacts. In such a world, the lines between working for others and running your own business have become blurred. For example, the pattern of working for someone else prior to starting a business, a trend now well established, appears to be the shortest road to owning your own business. Operating that business may not be the capstone of a career. Instead, it may be only the beginning of a whole new set of challenges.

BUILDING A BETTER MOUSETRAP

Many women are inspired by the fact that they can do something better than it is currently being done. They are driven to improve and expand upon existing ideas, technologies, products, or services. Their business is the way to accomplish this task.

Christine King[3]

Christine King is an example of the millions of female entrepreneurs who have created entirely new markets and can be described as innovation generals. As the mother of three school-age children, Christine became fed up with trying to shop and keep her kids occupied at the same time. And so in 1994 Christine launched Play 'n Store Products, Inc., a Cleveland manufacturer and distributor of "diversionary toys."

The products include small plastic tables with Lego®-like building blocks or interlocking gears and wall panels with funhouse mirrors and sliding beads. "If your kids are running down the aisle and rearranging the displays, you're worrying about their safety, and that diverts your attention from what you're buying," King says. "That's a problem."

In 2000 Play 'n Store generated $1 million in gross sales and Christine, 37, projects sales of $10 million by 2005. That projection seems conservative if the accounts she already has—including McDonald's, Blockbuster, Bally's Fitness, Stop and Shop, and Disney—continue to add her products in more locations. Christine says the climate is right for her product because baby-boomer parents often already feel guilty about working. "We're sure not going to get a baby-sitter all the time to run errands." Christine is proudest of the fact that she has created a niche where there was nothing before. "No one really does what we do," she says. "The opportunities are endless."

Leticia Herrera[4]

Leticia Herrera combined a love of buildings and fine architecture with a passion for art to create a company that would provide stone and metal restoration and cleaning services with the kind of skill and devotion usually reserved for fine works of art. Her company, now called ECI—formerly named Extra Clean, Inc.—faced an intensely competitive environment in the Chicago metropolitan area.

ECI has gone through several growth spurts and transformations. It began with just Leticia Herrera, two family members, and one contract for cleaning. She transformed the company from a fledgling underfunded janitorial company in a crowded marketplace into a specialty provider. After some success, she reinvented the firm to serve a highly specialized niche in fine stone and metal restoration and maintenance services.

In 11 years, her company grew to fifty employees with annual revenues close to $3 million. Her clients include the City of Chicago, the Museum of Science and Industry, the Shedd Aquarium, the Field Museum, the University of Illinois Chicago Campus, the Chicago Civic Opera House, and United Airlines. The company's best marketing plan was the quality of its reputation.

In her role as chairman, Letitia Herrera now oversees all phases of the firm's operations and plays an active part in working with clients to develop long-range preventive maintenance programs.

In building the ECI organization, Herrera assembled a team of geologists, metallurgists, sculptors, and other stone and metal specialists to make the company strengthen its place in the world of historic preservation, using procedures that are artistically sensitive, technically innovative, and environmentally safe.

Throughout her career, Herrera has been active in outreach work with the Latin American community. She takes seriously what she believes is her responsibility to "give back" to her community by delivering messages of economic empowerment, need for education, and the power of the Internet for breaking down borders and "leveling the playing field" for entrepreneurial ventures of all kinds.

Although she was motivated by several factors, her desire to fulfill her personal goals was the driving force behind the energy and enthusiasm for her business.

THE PRIDE OF ACHIEVEMENT

Extensive research into the characteristics of female entrepreneurs has established that the need for achievement is innate in many women. Those high in need for achievement are thought to have a general orientation toward certain types of goals, entrepreneurial activity being one.

Personal growth and self-determination—not attaining great wealth and building large operations—always rank high as motivating factors among women who have started their own businesses, according to Holly Buttner, a business faculty member at the University of North Carolina at Greensboro, who has spent four years in a study of female entrepreneurs. "Getting rich and owning a large company were not the major reasons these women started their own businesses; in fact, they didn't rank high as reasons. Profits were important, not so much as income, but as a means to ensure that the businesses they started would survive."[5] Buttner and Dorothy Moore, a business professor at the Citadel, Charleston, South Carolina, studied 129 women who had opened their own businesses in New York, Philadelphia, San Francisco, Chicago, Dallas, New Orleans, Boston, Cincinnati, and

Winston-Salem, North Carolina. The attitudes of the women they interviewed differ significantly from traditional notions of success. "My sense is that it was more than a money thing for most of the women who went into business for themselves," Buttner indicates. "It was a search for defining who they were and an opportunity to actualize their personal values in their work. Some of the women said if they had clients whose values differed significantly from theirs, they wouldn't work with them a second time. They wanted to choose who they worked with."

Among the kinds of companies started were financial consulting, computer training, insurance, catering, interior decorating, licensing copyright sales, new product development, consulting and planning, health and fitness, and retail sales. One woman has a business to help men improve their romantic life. Another does computer data conversion from one format to another. Others include making orthopedic shoes, designing apparel, and importing jewelry and crafts. "We did not see any large numbers of 'women's stereotype' businesses," Buttner points out. "They are in a variety of areas. There's nothing typical about the types of businesses that women are starting up."

Among measures of success, the women ranked commercial growth as one of the lowest, while personal growth was near the top. Business success traditionally has been measured in terms of sales and growth, but the entrepreneurs in the study didn't see these objectives as paramount. As one of the entrepreneurs noted, "You still have the same problems, you just tag on a zero or two to the bottom line" when the business grows.

Kristy Offineer[6]

Redbird's Journal is a culmination of eight years of research, planning, and dreaming for Kristy Offineer. Although it was obvious since college that she was headed for a career in journalism, the idea of owning and operating a Native American newspaper came about more slowly.

A member of the Oklahoma Cherokee, she grew up and was educated in Tulsa, Oklahoma. Her strong family connections developed during childhood visits with family friends throughout the city and rural Oklahoma. These trips with her parents fostered her awareness of the differences between life on and off the reservation. Her college years continued to sharpen her perception of Native American issues, all of which she felt helped her become uniquely qualified to edit a Native American newspaper.

Now with *Redbird Journal's* first and second issues behind her, Kristy says the response has been good. She is seeing a lot of interest in all tribes and tribal activities. Her publication's main focus is Native American events and issues, or as Kristy says, "Topics that affect us all." Having melded her personal heritage and passion with her journalism skills, Krsity is confident this combination will lead to her success. Millions of women like Kristy have started businesses with the same issue at the heart of their motivation. That is, to build a business that reflects their most profound passions and energies.

NOTES

1. From interview with authors, October 1999.

2. From the Web site of the National Association of Women Business Owners, www.nawbo.org.

3. From interview with authors, October 1999.

4. This story appeared on the Web site for the U.S. Small Business Administration's Women's Online Center, www.sba.gov.

5. From the United Nations Development Web site, www.undep.org.

6. This story appeared on the Web site for the U.S. Small Business Administration's Women's Online Center, www.sba.gov.

PART III

THE PROCESSES

8

The Challenges Facing Female Entrepreneurs

Obstacles are the stumbling blocks that often become the steppingstones to success.

Swahili saying

At a high-rise construction site in downtown Chicago, Judy DiAngelo, president and owner of Jade Carpentry Contractors, has just gotten off a temporary elevator running up the side of the building.

DiAngelo has been in the carpentry business only for about seven years. Before this, she was working as an executive with a major airline when she was passed over for a promotion in favor of a male colleague. Says Diangelo, "I was at a point in my life where I hit the glass ceiling in corporate America. And I really did hit it."[1]

DiAngelo decided she wanted to strike out on her own and start a business. Some of her family members were carpenters, so that seemed a natural direction to go. While about half of women-owned businesses are in the service sector, the number of women starting construction, agriculture, and manufacturing businesses has more than doubled in recent years.

DiAngelo says she soon found, whether she was trying to get loans from bankers or bidding on jobs from general contractors, she was running into walls because of her gender.

"There's an automatic assumption that every man knows what a hammer is and a screw and a nut. There . . . really is, in construction. You know, it's just automatic that these things are undecipherable to women."

Some other female business owners told DiAngelo of a place she could go to try to get help: the Women's Business Development Center in downtown Chicago, the largest nonprofit of its kind in the country. Over the past twelve years, it has provided services to some 20,000 women from a variety of socioeconomic backgrounds looking to start or expand their businesses.

The center's cofounder, Hedy Ratner, says 20,000 is actually a small number compared to what has been happening nationally. She calls today the golden age of entrepreneurship for women. "Right now, there are nine million women-owned businesses in the United States. Those women-owned businesses have generated $3.6 trillion in sales and employed one of every four U.S. company workers, a total of over 18 million employees. So, what we're talking about is an enormous growth, an explosion."

Over the years, Ratner has become a crusader for women entrepreneurs. She organizes a conference every year, bringing thousands of women from around the country together with politicians, corporate representatives, and community leaders. President William Clinton appointed her to the National Women's Business Council to work on policy recommendations. Ratner says, despite the recent boom in woman-owned businesses, a host of challenges still face woman entrepreneurs.

FEMALE ENTREPRENEURS AND THE CHALLENGES THEY FACE

In the industrialized world, an intimidating statistic for any would-be female entrepreneur is that more than half of all startups will fail within five years. The question immediately raised is, why is the failure rate so high?

Troy A. Festervand and Jack E. Forrest are professors at Middle Tennessee University who study entrepreneurship. They also have directed small business development centers, and they have identified the three biggest mistakes entrepreneurs make: undercapitalizing the business, going into business for the wrong reasons, and failing to put together a solid business model.

"Just because you have enough money to rent a building and buy a little inventory, that's not proper capitalization," says Festervand.

"Just because you have a hobby, it doesn't mean that it's a valid business idea. And just being a nice person doesn't qualify as a good business model."[2]

What does a successful female entreprenuer need to do? Festervand recommends these three steps:

- *Build up your reserves.* Festervand says that you should have at least six months of working capital in the bank before you launch a business. Make sure you have enough money to pay your bills and manage your debt so that it will not exceed 50 percent of revenues. Put together a budget with the help of a local small business development center or other, noncompeting small businesses in your area. "Those are the people who can give you the real skinny on what it's going to cost to do business," says Festervand.[3]

- *Don't do it on a whim.* Why start a business? It's a simple question, but one for which many female entrepreneurs don't have a good answer. Festervand has heard every reason in the book: You're unhappy in your current job; you don't feel challenged; you got laid off; you're going through a midlife crisis. "Too often, it's predicated too much on emotion rather than common sense, logic, things that can be justified," he says. "That's not to say that emotions don't play a large role in the decision. That final leap is an emotional thing. But there's a difference between that last step being an emotional thing and the entire startup process being an emotional response." What's a good reason for starting a business? You've identified a need for the product or service you want to provide.[4]

- *Picture it.* Imagine yourself running the business. What will you have to do every day? How many employees will you need to hire, and what tasks will they perform? If you've worked for a large corporation all your life, this may be a tough leap, and so you need a game plan, says Festervand. "Do you have a recipe for how you're going to run this business?" he asks. "The term 'business plan' is overused these days, but most people who prepare a meal use recipes. I realize there are lots of great cooks who don't require recipes. But not inexperienced ones." Make sure you have the skills necessary to run the business. If you don't, get them. Then put your plan down on paper.

While these seem like logical steps, many aspiring female entrepreneurs simply don't think through the decision. "It would be analogous to saying, 'I'm going to take off for New York without a roadmap; I'm just going to head in that direction,' " says Festervand of skipping over the planning stage. "I guess you can get there, but a far more efficient approach would be to lay out your path beforehand."[5]

Hedy Ratner adds that the first thing a woman ought to consider is whether she really wants to do this. She suggests asking yourself, "Are you really the entrepreneurial person? Are you willing to generate eighteen hours a day, seven days a week for the first couple of years? Are you willing to put every penny you've got into the development of a business? Are you willing to manage the finances of your business? Or forget about any social interest for the next year, because you're going to be working as hard as you possibly can to just get to eat? And then maybe you'll start making money, and maybe you won't."

Ratner agrees that one of the biggest problems for any new female business is getting access to capital. And she says this is especially true for women. She says things have been getting better in recent years. The Small Business Administration has been working to guarantee more loans for women. And some banks, sensing a growing market, are even actively looking for women entrepreneurs. Ratner helps women find these banks.

Some bankers in Chicago say they are more likely to fund a business if the women running it are getting training and guidance from a group like Hedy Ratner's. Of course, Ratner says some loan officers are just resistant to the idea of lending to women. She doesn't just blame the bankers. It is not just the fault of the banks. It is also the fault of the women seeking the loans.

Ratner says sometimes women will not put together as thorough a business plan as their male counterparts. She says often that's because they don't have the resources and relationships that men have. Ratner says they need to seek out those resources. "You have to—to present yourself as professionally and seriously as you want to be taken. If you want to be taken seriously, you'd better come in with a serious proposal and a serious loan package. That's crucial."[6]

It may seem on the surface that many of the challenges faced by female entrepreneurs are similar to those faced by their male counterparts. There is one challenge, however, that is unquestionably salient for women business owners. The challenge is as old as biology itself: the difficulty of balancing a fledgling company and a fledgling family. Whether it is in Miami or Moscow or Mumbai, female entrepreneurs the world over struggle over how to be both a great mother and CEO.

ARE WOMEN ENTREPRENEURS MORE LIKELY TO FAIL THAN MEN?

Now given the tough road many female entrepreneurs face, one might think that women business owners run a distant second to their male counterparts, right? Don't be so sure.

In the United States and Western Europe, long gone are the days when woman-owned businesses were viewed as minor-league operations. As we have previously discussed, the sheer scope and scale of female-owned companies in these countries has skyrocketed in recent years. Many of the women starting businesses today aren't individuals who just want to stay at home and start a little something on the side. Instead, their businesses are getting bigger and more substantial.

Worldwide, men still make up the majority of people who start and own their own businesses. Men are often motivated by a drive that often stems from disagreements with their bosses or a feeling they can run things better. For men, the transition from a past occupation to the new venture is often facilitated when the new venture is an outgrowth of a present job. Women, on the other hand, often leave a previous occupation with only a high level of enthusiasm for the new venture rather than experience, making the transition more difficult. Startup financing is another area where male and female entrepreneurs differ. While males often list investors and bank loans in addition to personal funds as sources of startup capital, women usually rely solely on personal assets or savings.

Occupationally, there are differences between male and female entrepreneurs. Men more often are recognized specialists in their fields or have attained competence in a variety of business skills. Their experience is often in manufacturing, finance, or technical areas. Most women, in contrast, usually have administrative experience, usually in more service-related areas such as education, secretarial work, or retail sales. The result is often smaller female-owned businesses with lower net earnings.

There are strong similarities in personality between male and female entrepreneurs. Both tend to be energetic, goal-oriented, and independent. Men are often more confident and less flexible and tolerant than women, which can result in different management styles driving the new venture.

Despite these differences, a new study suggests that businesses owned by women often generate just as many sales, experience just as much employee growth, and enjoy just as much profitability as those owned by men.[7]

"I've been researching in this field since the 1980s, and it always used to be imagined that men did better," says Robert D. Hisrich, Mixon Chaired Professor of Entrepreneurship at Case Western University and the study's author. "Indeed, they don't differ as much as you might think. I'm very excited about that finding."

According to the study, released by RISEbusiness, the Research Institute for Small and Emerging Business, Inc., in Washington, D.C., women have different business styles, strategies, and cultures. And those differences can have profound effects on the companies they run.

Hisrich made several surprising—and other not-so-surprising—findings.

More experience means fewer employees. The more years of work experience a woman has, the less likely she is to grow her employee base. Hisrich says that's largely because these women generally launch their companies later in life, after they've worked for years in the corporate world. They often want to keep the business small, as a sort of stop on the road to retirement.

Quantitative skills do not translate into employee growth. Women with high quantitative skills are also unlikely candidates for large employee bases. "The only explanation I can think of for that is the type of businesses they form," says Hisrich. "They start companies that have less propensity to grow."

Women aren't as big on families as you might think. Despite the general consensus that women are more family-friendly, men pay much more for employee benefits—$3,561 per employee more.

Women seem to be hitching their fortunes to the entrepreneurial spirit in the air, writing their own business plans and appointing themselves president and CEO. Myra Hart, a professor of entrepreneurship at Harvard Business School observes "They're going straight out on their own. The economic environment is better for women than ever before."[8]

Women sacrifice for the firm. Men take much higher personal salaries, which Hisrich says could be attributed to the fact that male respondents were an average of ten years older than their female counterparts.

Women take business personally. Women say they are better at managing human resources, communicating orally and in written form, and developing personal relationships.

Hisrich says he hopes to take these findings and expand upon them in future studies. He'd like to look at how women create, develop, and implement business strategies, as well as how those strategies affect their success.

"Women entrepreneurs today are a significant factor in the U.S. economy, so we hope we can get funding and be in the field within three months," he says. "I think that once we recognize that women are very successful entrepreneurs who can grow and be equally good in sales and profits, that definitely should help change things. And it has changed."

CHALLENGES FACING FEMALE ENTREPRENEURS OUTSIDE THE UNITED STATES

The recognition of the needs and characteristics of female entrepreneurs has led many forward-thinking organizations to take the initiative and help female entrepreneurs overcome the roadblocks before them.

According to the Finnish Ministry of Development, unemployment in the Kymenlaakso region in southeast Finland rose alarmingly from 5.4 percent to 20 percent between 1990 and 1993. In response, the government launched a number of initiatives to reverse this trend, and one of the most ambitious has been to encourage women to set up their own companies. The New Jobs for Women project, launched in the region in 1996, provides women with six months of training in entrepreneurship. The scheme is backed by the European Social Fund, the Kotka and Hamina employment offices and district enterprise services, the Kymi labor district, banks, the Kotka and Hamina vocational training institutes, and several other partners. During the 1996–98 period, eighty women were trained; about 80 percent of them either became entrepreneurs or worked in other people's businesses. The training—targeted at unemployed women over 25 years old—also includes four weeks of work in a participating company.

The course begins by examining the psychological demands of entrepreneurship. Project manager Helena Lönnroth says that it helps the trainees understand their own values as well. "At the end of the first phase each participant has an understanding of her qualifications as an entrepreneur," she says. "The participants learn marketing, cost calculation, legal and social issues. The entrepreneur must understand the administrative and economic environment in which she works."

By September 1997 twenty-two of the thirty-two initial participants, or almost 70 percent, had set up their own businesses (often in areas like tourism, restaurants, handicrafts, or health care), applied for other training courses, or otherwise found a job.

As part of the project, the Women's Resource Center was established in the city of Hamina in 1996 to provide information and assistance for new entrepreneurs setting up in the Kymenlaakso region. Center manager Leena Jantunen says that women have used the premises and equipment to get started by using facilities to produce business cards and information brochures.

Soon after the resource center was established, a number of local artisans set up a handicraft cooperative to sell their products with the center's help. According to Lönnroth, this has proved particularly important for women who do handicraft work on top of regular jobs. "They don't always have the courage to set up their own business. But they can sell their products in the handicraft shop either by joining the co-operative or by working on a commission basis."

Another course participant, Pia Pentti, a mother of five, said she found the self-analysis a real shock. "I had to look at myself again, and ask questions about who I really am," she said. Soon after completing the course, Pia bought a dressmaker's store in Hamina and transformed it into a handicraft shop. "The training course gave me the courage to believe in my own skills," she says.

Starting a business can be an enticing dream to a Canadian woman, especially if you're a woman crouching under a corporate glass ceiling or a recent graduate skeptical about salaried work. The number of self-employed women in Canada grew 42.4 percent between 1992 and 1997, compared with about 22.1 percent for men, according to Statistics Canada, a government research agency.

For many women, the dream ends abruptly when they're faced with the average income for self-employed women (both full- and part-time): about $8,000, as measured by Statistics Canada in 1997. This was slightly more than half the amount earned by self-employed men.

Clearly, women operate smaller and less profitable businesses than those owned by men—regardless of industry sector or age of their firm. In absolute dollar terms, woman-owned businesses simply do not grow as much or as fast. New research helps us understand why.

The question of why some businesses grow and others don't is the theme of a multimillion-dollar, cross-Canada research initiative housed at the University of British Columbia.

The Experience Gap

Women tend to bring less management-related experience to their businesses. While the study finds that men and women business owners are, on average, equally well educated, women have fewer financial and marketing management skills. This partially reflects the fact that women are concentrated at lower levels in most organizations, with less opportunity to gain management experience.

These differences show up in the way they run their businesses. Women owners in Canada tended to focus on internal administration (such as management and financial planning) while a comparative sample of male business owners was more actively engaged in those activities associated with growth—joint venturing, exporting, and product development.

These differences have an impact on business survival. Professors Eileen Fischer at York University and Becky Reuber at the University of Toronto have found that a company is more likely to survive when its owner has been exposed to a wide variety of management tasks and is better able to cope with the unexpected. Breadth of experience matters more than length. The lessons here are that would-be entrepreneurs should focus on acquiring a range of management skills—whether through jobs or courses. Business owners who lack broad experience would be well advised to seek partners, mentors, employees, and boards of advisers who can complement their own backgrounds.

The Attitude Gap

Many Canadian business owners simply do not want their firms to grow, an attitude more characteristic of women, according to the Carleton study, which found that after five years, only half the female entrepreneurs in Canada were seeking growth, compared to 70 percent of the men.

What's behind this gap? The study found that men are more likely to want to expand their firms because of their need for respect, earnings, and control of their work environment. Canadian women, on the other hand, are more influenced by the need to balance work and family, their contributions to their neighborhoods and local networks, and the opinions of their significant others—all factors that can dissuade them from expanding.

Evening the Odds

Findings like these are helping trainers and female business owners themselves in Canada to grapple with growth. Patti Sullivan, executive director of the Manitoba Women's Enterprise Centre in Winnipeg, has used research to improve her programs for clients.

"We've modified our information sessions and created special training events that help expose clients to a broader range of business topics. In April of 2000, we took another step by hosting an international conference for women in business. Women throughout the country met with a broad range of business owners in order to self-assess the management skills they need to foster business growth."

In many ways, gender does affect the way women do business. We have heard many women business owners express frustration that they are not always taken seriously. This frustration is coupled with the challenge of building professional credibility and business contacts with comparatively less management experience.

On the other hand, findings from a 1999 Department of Foreign Affairs and International Trade study suggest that some women entrepreneurs are losing no time fostering growth—and survival—of their businesses. In the largest study in the world of women entrepreneurs who export, researchers found that a high proportion of woman-owned firms in Canada export early in their life cycle, many at startup. This group of women represents an emerging wave of more experienced managers who understand that exporting is essential for growth.[9]

Emmie Leung[10]

"It was pure desperation," says Emmie Leung of her decision to start her recycling business, within months of graduation from the University of Manitoba back in 1976. "I was a woman, a visible minority with little English and no business experience. The job offers were very scarce." The best course seemed to be to start a business—in an industry no one had ever heard of. "Somehow, that seemed safest," she says with a laugh.

Against her father's wishes, Leung had moved to Canada in 1972 to pursue a business degree. "I was expected to marry and raise a family," she says, "and it was made very clear he would not help me financially and I would not be welcomed back." So, with $15,000 in savings, she moved to Vancouver and convinced local municipalities to participate in her curious plan to collect and recycle their waste newspaper and, later, plastic, glass, and tin. The idea was so novel, she remembers, her business license was filed under the category of junk dealer. "In Asia, we reuse everything we can; I could better see the waste in wasting waste."

In the early days, CEO Leung's was a one-woman operation. In her truck she picked up bundles of newspaper; she sorted the materials by hand at her small warehouse; she tinkered with the machines she used to compact and bale the paper; she doggedly marketed her compacted paper and pulverized glass and tin to manufacturers in Canada and overseas; she even mopped the floors. "Those were the best times," she recalls wistfully. "It was very seat-of-the-pants."

Today, IPI employs more than 100 people at four processing facilities in the Vancouver area and generates annual earnings of $12 to $15 million. Leung's success has won her father's blessing. Now her challenge is competition—the large corporations that have since recognized the value in waste products. "There may be an initial reward for being a pioneer in an industry, but after that, you're on your own, yet again."

NOTES

1. Crain's Chicago Business, "Up and Out," November 21, 1998.

2. Small Business Depot.com, "Why Entrepreneurs Fail," www.sbdepot.com, August 11, 2000.

3. Ibid.

4. Ibid.

5. Ibid.

6. Crain's Chicago Business, "Up and Out," November 21, 1998.

7. Robert D. Hisrich and Candida Brush, *Women vs. Men Entrepreneurs: A Comparative Study* (Washington, D.C.: RISEbusiness, 1999).

8. Ibid.

9. *Beyond Borders: Canadian Businesswomen in International Trade* (Toronto, Ont.: Canadian Department of Foreign Affairs and International Trade, 1999).

10. Christine Hanlon, "Garbage Guru," from the web site of the University of Manitoba (Alumni Association), www.umanitoba.com.

9

Tools and Processes for Helping Female Entrepreneurs

Long range planning does not deal with future decisions, but with the future of present decisions.[1]

Peter Drucker

For many female entrepreneurs, the right advice can make all the difference. Almost universally, it seems the minute a woman starts her business, everyone is trying to give her advice. Suddenly, everybody—friends, family, acquaintances, bankers, small-business counselors—are offering their "wisdom" on what the female entrepreneur should and should not do. For the uninitiated, the plethora of opinions and ideas can be overwhelming and, at times, dangerous.

In order to wade through all the information at her disposal, the female entrepreneur does best to first systematically evaluate her personal needs. We call this assessing the internal entrepreneur. Then, with this knowledge in place, she can more realistically and comprehensively seek out and work with potential help givers. In this chapter, we will detail a personal assessment for prospective female entrepreneurs. In chapter 10 we will provide strategies for locating and evaluating a potential help giver.

ASSESSING THE INTERNAL ENTREPRENEUR

The first step in the assessment is to make an honest appraisal of the female entrepreneur's personal skills and abilities. This is a critical step, which many would-be entrepreneurs skip. The most important role a help-giving organization can take is helping the female entrepreneur conduct an accurate and objective appraisal of her strengths and weaknesses.

In the developed world, especially the United States, entrepreneurship is a goal for many individuals, men and women alike. Being an entrepreneur is part of the "American Dream." Help-giving organizations in the United States, like the Small Business Development Centers, actually try in many cases to discourage potential entrepreneurs. Very often the potential business owner lacks a realistic appreciation of the risk involved and the many years of hard work required before the business will become profitable. Most startups also underestimate the amount of money that will be required to finance the early years in business. Too many swallow the myth that owning a business is the fastest way to become wealthy.

Help-giving organizations in countries with transition economies like Poland try to create programs that will encourage the spirit of entrepreneurship. Individuals who were raised and worked in an environment where business ownership was either discouraged or simply not a part of the social or business culture need to be educated and sold on the idea of entrepreneurship. In these countries women may need more encouragement to start businesses and more help developing confidence in their ability to become entrepreneurs.

BEHAVIORAL ASSESSMENT

Several excellent instruments are available to help a woman identify her strengths and weaknesses. One that is particularly helpful for prospective entrepreneurs is the DISC Behavioral Profile.

Organizations mentioned in Appendix I may offer self-evaluation instruments to prospective entrepreneurs, as do many management consultants. Libraries that have career-planning collections may also offer behavioral profiling. The DISC profile in Figure 9.1 gives a detailed analysis of four areas of a person's behavioral style.

The first is her problem-solving style—is she an assertive, aggressive problem solver or a conservative, calculating problem solver? The assertive problem solver would be referred to as a conductor. The

Figure 9.1
Evaluating the Female Entrepreneur's DISC Behavioral Style

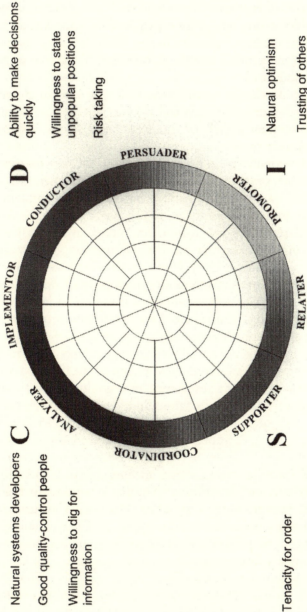

SUCCESS INSIGHTS WHEEL™

D
Ability to make decisions quickly

Willingness to state unpopular positions

Risk taking

I
Natural optimism

Trusting of others

Ability to make others feel welcomed or included

C
Natural systems developers

Good quality-control people

Willingness to dig for information

S
Tenacity for order

Natural ability to organize tasks

Record-keeping skills

conductor entrepreneur will be competitive, driving, and strong-willed. Her strengths will be the areas of sales and negotiation. She will be a fast and aggressive problem solver with a high tolerance for risk. Starting and growing a business requires extensive decision making, and the style of decision making will set the tone for the future of the business.

It is important for every entrepreneur to identify understand their "blind spots." Then they can surround themselves with individuals who compensate for their weaknesses. The primary weaknesses for the conductor entrepreneur, for example, are taking action too quickly without considering all the consequences and turning people off with their demanding style.

The second area evaluated by the DISC profile is the woman's influencing style. Is she an extroverted, optimistic person or an introverted, pessimistic person? The extroverted influencer would be referred to as a promoter. The promoter entrepreneur will be optimistic, fast-paced, enthusiastic, and persuasive. Strengths of the promoter entrepreneur include motivating employees, servicing customers, and selling, all of which require a person to be friendly, optimistic, and comfortable dealing with people. Two of the weaknesses of the promoter entrepreneur are her high trust level, which may lead to being taken advantage of, and disorganization that comes from taking on too much too soon.

The third element of DISC measures the prospective entrepreneur's preference for pace and reaction to change. Is she laid back, process oriented, and resistant to change (low risk), or does she prefer a fast pace and lots of change and variety (high risk)? The slower-paced, process-oriented person would be referred to as a supporter. The supporter entrepreneur is patient, consistent, and steady. Her strengths would be in the areas of business that require thoughtful review, including technology, accounting, and operations. Running an entrepreneurial company requires an ability to react quickly to changes in technology and the marketplace. The supporter entrepreneur has a high need for consistency and predictability. They need to be supported by individuals who can guide and assist them through the change process.

And last, DISC measures how a person responds to rules and procedures. Is the prospective entrepreneur a precise, analytical person who follows rules, or does she prefer to make the rules up as she goes? The precise rule-oriented person would be referred to as an analyzer. The analyzer entrepreneur is careful, exacting, systematic, and neat. She often comes from a technical career in engineering, finance, or technology. While her strengths are clearly in the technical areas of the business, she is also good at planning and developing realistic projections because of her critical nature. Her weakness is just the flip side of her strength—at times she will be too slow to act, overanalytical, and too critical of herself and others.

Running a business requires talents from throughout the behavioral spectrum. The person handling the finances or technical aspects of the business will need the analytical skills. On the other hand, selling, strategic planning, and problem solving for customers will require an ability to "make it up as they go." No one person has all the necessary strengths, so the solution is to identify what should be delegated to either key employees or outside resources such as consultants.

ASSESSMENT OF BUSINESS AND INDUSTRY EXPERIENCE

The prospective business owner also needs to be clear on her strengths and weaknesses for starting and growing a business. As she evaluates her strengths and weaknesses, she should weigh them against her experience with all aspects of running a business, including bookkeeping and accounting, sales and marketing, hiring and managing employees, negotiating and buying products, managing inventory, and operations. Often the overlooked but most important skill is the ability to sell. Hardly a business exists in which the owner is the not the primary salesperson. Many entrepreneurs have a passion and desire about their service or product but forget they'll have to sell to someone in order to have a business.

A study quoted in the *Wall Street Journal* shows the backgrounds of women entrepreneurs: 25 percent from management, 21 percent from sales, 18 percent from accounting or finance, 6 percent from marketing, 4 percent from engineering, 3 percent from human resources, and 23 percent other backgrounds.[2]

The new generation of women entrepreneurs appears to be better equipped for success than those of two decades earlier. Women who started or acquired their firms within the past ten years are more highly educated than women who have owned their firms for twenty or more years and have more management experience.

Fully 45 percent of women who have become business owners in the past decade have at least a bachelor's degree, compared to just 26 percent of those who have been in business for twenty years or more.

Among the new generation of women business owners, 38 percent held an executive, senior-, or middle-management position before their entrepreneurial careers, compared to just 20 percent of women who have owned their firms for twenty years or more.[3]

"The great news here is that the new generation of women entrepreneurs is more likely to have started a business that is related to their previous career. Over half (51%) of those who started their firms within the past 10 years indicate their business is closely related to their previous career, compared to 33% of those who started their firms 20 or more years ago," said Myra Hart, vice chair of the Center for Women's Business Research and a Harvard Business School professor. "This is positive because we know that the more closely related the business is to the owner's previous work experience, the greater the likelihood of success."

The female entrepreneur should also assess her knowledge of the industry she is contemplating joining. She should list what she knows about the field or industry, concentrating on specific business information and general life experience. All experience will be useful when making a decision about what skills she may need to develop in order to run her business. The sample business plan in Appendix II outlines the information that a prospective entrepreneur will need to know about her business and industry.

It is helpful for the female entrepreneur to evaluate and understand the whys and hows of what she has accomplished up to this point in her life so that she can better use the knowledge to her advantage. The following questions will help her do this. The more honestly she can answer the questions, the more useful the information will be to her:

• What are her main strengths?
• What are her weaknesses?
• How would someone else answer the above two questions?
• What talents does she possess and in what situations has she been able to use them?

DETERMINING FINANCIAL REQUIREMENTS

In order to start her own business, it is important for the female entrepreneur to consider her financial situation. By determining current income and expenses, she will be better at projecting her financial needs for the startup phase and beyond.

For most small businesses, there is a gap between starting the business and producing income. In fact, most management consultants who specialize in small businesses suggest that a female entrepreneur have at least six months of savings available for the startup phase of her business. Of course, this number will vary with the type of business. In fact, many businesses take up to five years to produce a positive cash flow. Service businesses and home-based businesses are a favorite choice for many women because the startup costs are considerably lower than for other businesses.

Before the female entrepreneur makes the decision whether to go into business, she needs to develop a personal plan of saving and spending. This will help her identify how much money she needs each month in order to live. It will also tell her if the dream of owning her own business fits with other dreams such as sending a child to college. To develop a personal saving and spending plan, female entrepreneurs should

- First, identify and write down fixed expenses for each month for the next year. Fixed expenses include such things as insurance, housing, car payments, utilities, and savings.
- Once all the fixed expenses for each month have been identified, add up the monthly fixed expenses and compute annual fixed expenses.
- Next, identify flexible expenses and write them down for each month over the next year. The female entrepreneur should consider what she has spent in previous months and any changes she might wish to consider. Flexible expenses include such things as food (including dining in restaurants), clothing and personal care, entertainment, and transportation (gas).
- Once all flexible expenses for each month have been identified, add up the monthly flexible expenses and calculate annual flexible expenses.
- Now subtract total fixed expenses and total flexible expenses for each month and the year from expected monthly and annual income.

After examining savings and spending requirements, the prospective female entrepreneur may find that she lacks the necessary resources to start her business. In fact, this may be the first obstacle that she will need to overcome.

Approximately 75 percent of women business owners use their personal savings to start their businesses. However, if they need more than they have in their savings accounts, other money sources may be available from bank loans, family members, partners, friends, venture capital companies, property to mortgage, loans from the government, or organizations dedicated to supporting female entrepreneurs. In a study by the National Foundation for Women Business Owners, it was found that 23 percent of women business owners financed the growth of their companies by using credit cards.[4]

Many of the organizations listed in Appendix I either directly or indirectly provide financial resources or information to prospective female entrepreneurs. A good rule of thumb is that the female entrepreneur should not borrow more money than is necessary to start her business. The more money that is borrowed, the less control she will have.

PERSONAL GOAL SETTING

Personal goal setting is crucial when deciding whether to start a business. Because her business will have an impact on every other area of her life, it is critical to know how it fits into her life and whether it allows her to reach her other goals. Two of the benefits a prospective female entrepreneur will receive as a result of defining and aligning her major goals in life are peace of mind and focus. A few of the other benefits of personal goal setting for the prospective female entrepreneur:

• Make better decisions
• Be more organized and effective
• Have greater confidence and self-worth

A female entrepreneur will not pay a price for setting goals, but she will pay a price for not setting them. Clear-cut goals and objectives help to maintain focus and purpose. A woman will need to evaluate her goals and the validity of them by asking the following questions:

• Is the goal really achievable?
• Does the goal stretch my capabilities?
• Is it morally right and fair?
• Are my short-range goals consistent with my long-term goals?
• Can I commit myself emotionally to completing the project?
• Can I visualize myself reaching this goal?

The prospective female entrepreneur needs to set long-range and short-term goals. Long-range goals may help to overcome short-range failures. People who set ambitious long-range goals have been found to have higher self-confidence, higher self-esteem, and greater personal motivation. There are seven steps that the prospective female entrepreneur should go through to set each goal for her business. To be effective, each goal should include all seven of the following steps:

- Identify the goal by writing it down.
- Set a deadline for the achievement. Put a date on it.
- List the obstacles to overcome in accomplishing the goal.
- Identify the people and groups whose cooperation is needed to reach the goal.
- List the skills and knowledge required to reach the goal. What do you need to know?
- Develop a plan of action to reach the goal.
- Write down the benefits of achieving the goal. ("What is in it for me?")

It is important to reevaluate goals periodically to make certain that they still are in alignment with personal values and goals.

IS NOW THE RIGHT TIME?

Overall, specialists who study small business startups have found that the most important characteristics for success include

- Knowledge in the field from both formal training and on-the-job experience
- Attitude or willingness to work long hours for many months and sometimes years, without expecting much income
- A business plan—a business without a plan is a ship without a rudder
- Capital, cash, resources
- Action—implementation—get it done

If the prospective female entrepreneur has come to the point where she feels comfortable with her self-assessment on those characteristics, it is a good sign she is ready to move forward. If she feels weak on one or more points, she may want to ask herself if now is the right time.

A personal assessment that evaluates behavioral style, business expertise, industry knowledge, finances, and personal goals is vitally important for any prospective female entrepreneur to undertake. Once the female entrepreneur has a firm grasp and knowledge of herself, her goals, and her abilities, she can move on to the next stage of business development, which is finding and evaluating help givers and developing her business plan.

NOTES

1. *Quotes and Quips* (Salt Lake City, Utah: Covey Leadership Center, 1993), p. 51.

2. "Women Entrepreneurship Statistics," Wall Street Journal, date unknown.

3. *The New Generation of Women Business Owners: An Executive Report* (Washington, D.C.: Center for Women's Business Research, 2001), underwritten by First Union Corporation.

4. "Women Business Owners Make Progress in Access to Capital" (Washington D.C., National Foundation for Women Business Owners, 1996).

Locating and Evaluating Potential Help Givers

> At times, it is as hard to see oneself as to look backwards without turning around.
>
> Henry David Thoreau

The number of potential help givers for female entrepreneurs is growing rapidly all over the world. Appendix I details governmental and nongovernmental organizations that are dedicated to fostering female entrepreneurship. Although we feel the list is extensive, many worthy organizations may have been inadvertently left off. We apologize to any that might have been. Nevertheless, the appendix provides a reliable starting point for many female entrepreneurs as they seek out help givers.

Help givers are not only potential financial sources but also providers of information and knowledge. The number of help givers can overwhelm; the prospective female entrepreneur should properly evaluate the possibilities.

CLEARLY IDENTIFY NEEDS

Before a female entrepreneur can begin to evaluate potential help givers, she must be clear about the type and depth of help she needs. She will likely seek both personal and organizational help. In order to gain the maximum benefit from the help giver, a woman must have clear-cut objectives.

In Chapter 9 we overviewed an assessment process for the female business owner. Many organizations offer the female business owner help in improving her personal skills. Training and individual coaching will help women address the issues they identify from their assessment. Many help-giving organizations also offer training for skills such as time management or communication. Fortunately, many of the organizations that help women with their personal challenges understand the importance of offering motivation and encouragement. Starting and growing a business is often a lonely and isolating experience. Providing emotional and social help is as important as providing operational assistance.

Second, the women business owner must squarely understand the organizational assistance she requires. Appendix II gives a sample business plan. It is critical that a women business owner spend the time to write a business plan before she approaches a potential help giver. The process of writing the business plan will force her to evaluate her existing business or new business idea with a critical eye. When starting a new business there are many issues that need to be addressed and projects to be undertaken. Success comes from putting resources into those projects that will yield the greatest return.

A business plan is also an absolute must for any female entrepreneur who is going to be seeking financing. Banks, venture capitalists, and government agencies will look to the business plan as proof that the female entrepreneur is serious and realistically understands her risks. There are many organizations that offer support to the female business owner in developing her business plan. For instance, the Council of Smaller Enterprises in Cleveland, Ohio, which is the largest small-business organization in the United States, sponsors a yearly business plan contest. Participants in the program receive training and support to develop their plan. There are several categories of winners, with the top winner receiving a cash award of $50,000 along with numerous services such free tax preparation, legal advice, and even coffee service for a year.

FINANCIAL SUPPORT

For the women business owner who is seeking capital, many organizations have come into existence in recent years that are designed to connect the business owner with potential investors. Kay Kiplovitz, founder and former CEO of USA Networks, started Springboard, a nonprofit series of investment forums intended to link venture capitalists with female entrepreneurs. Her efforts have led to more than $400 million in venture financing for women. VentureOne, a venture capital research firm, reports that only 4.43 percent of the $68.8 billion in venture capital in 2001 went to companies whose chief executives were women.[1]

The key to competing for funds is having a good plan and being able to effectively present the plan to potential investors. Often this requires assistance either from professionals such as accountants, bankers, or attorneys or from other women business owners who act as mentors.

Institutional equity investors report that two-thirds (64 percent) of the proposals that they seriously consider come from referral networks, and that only one-third (36 percent) are unsolicited. Referred proposals come primarily from attorneys (45 percent), accountants and CPAs (33 percent), other equity investment firms (29 percent), and word of mouth (27 percent).[2]

THE ROLE MENTORS CAN PLAY

More and more, organizations that support female entrepreneurs are actively encouraging current members to mentor prospective business owners. Although mentor matching can be a time-consuming program to organize and manage, it is one of the best ways to assist the new or prospective business owner.

Mentors are experienced women business owners willing to give back to their communities by assisting other women ready to start or grow their businesses. Mentors can also come from legal, financial, or other professions, providing guidance, advice, and training to women entrepreneurs. Mentors act as trusted counselors and share their business knowledge, skills, and experience and, most important, serve as respected role models.

A mentor is the one person in front of whom every question is a good question and in front of whom it is acceptable to be uninformed—as long as the woman business owner is attempting to learn. Having a mentor is one of the best ways for a new entrepreneur to learn about starting and growing a business.

BENEFITS OF MENTORING

An effective mentor can provide

- A nonthreatening learning opportunity
- Encouragement to confront challenges, seize opportunities, overcome problems, recognize weaknesses, and build on strengths
- Networking and partnership opportunities
- Coaching and constructive feedback
- Business expertise to assist in decision making

Women business owners are less likely than their male counterparts to have a mentor before opening a business but are more likely to consult outside sources on business management and growth issues, according to a survey from the National Foundation for Women Business Owners (NFWBO).[3] The study was sponsored by a collaboration of nonprofit foundations, the Edward Lowe Foundation, and the Kauffman Center for Entrepreneurial Leadership in conjunction with FleetBoston Financial.

When owners of fast-growth firms were starting or acquiring their firms, less than half the women had a mentor or role model. "Women who own fast-growing businesses are also less likely than men who own fast-growing firms to indicate that someone close to them was an entrepreneur when they were growing up," according to Mark Lange, executive director of the Edward Lowe Foundation. "Only 43% of fast-growth women owners had an entrepreneurial role model, compared to 59% of fast-growth men owners."

Women may compensate for the lack of mentors by consulting more with outside sources while they grow their businesses. "Gaining new perspectives from outside sources on business management and growth issues is an important ingredient in expanding a business," noted Lange. "Sixty percent of the fast-growth women owners consult with accountants compared to 44% of men owners of fast-growing firms. Furthermore, women owners of fast-growing firms are the most likely to discuss business issues with their family and fellow business owners."

NETWORKING

Another very effective method for the women business owner to get assistance in developing her plan is networking. Networks foster self-help, exchange information, improve productivity, and share resources. The primary goal of many help-giving organizations is to create a network for the woman business owner. The concept behind networking is that a group of individuals forms relationships based on common interests, and members later help each other in the form of contacts, leads, or advice. Women have been excluded from some traditionally male networks in the past. Many private clubs where men networked prohibited women from membership. Women have also at times found it difficult to establish relationships in predominantly male networks, because of the impression that the network was "closed." Hence the success of the many organizations who offer networking exclusively to women.

GROUP PURCHASING

The good news for potential women business owners is that more and more large corporations are actively seeking them out to assist them in their startup stage and provide them with cost-saving benefits. Large companies know that businesses owned by women are growing faster than the economy in general. Woman-owned businesses are growing in number and economic clout. Between 1992 and 1997, the number of woman-owned firms increased 16 percent, employment expanded 28 percent, and revenues grew 33 percent.

Clearly women business owners are a profitable market for large companies to target. As an example, the National Association of Women Business Owners (NAWBO), one of the largest organizations for women business owners in the United States, offers sponsorship opportunities to companies wanting to sell to female entrepreneurs. The list of NAWBO sponsors includes AT&T, Jaguar, Kemper Insurance, Principal Financial Group, UPS, Wells Fargo, Wyndham Hotels, Avis, and MBNA Bank, just to name a few. Members of NAWBO can utilize the benefits offered by these companies, which may include discounts or special programs targeted toward the women business owner. For example, another sponsor, Copy Systems, Inc., offers NAWBO members a 30 percent discount on several models of copiers, fax machines, and laser printers.

EVALUATING HELP GIVERS

The first step in evaluating an organization is to review what their primary focus is, and whether it matches the needs of the woman business owner. Does the organization focus primarily on lending money or on business education, for example? Following is a list of questions to consider in the evaluation of a help-giving organization:

- Why does the organization exist?
- What is their mission statement?
- What are their sources of funding?
- Why do the funding sources give to this organization?
- What types of female entrepreneurs do they work with?
- What industries do they focus on?
- Do they lend money or have relationships with entities that do?
- What kind of startup counseling do they provide?
- Do they provide leadership and management training?
- Do they provide a mentoring program?
- What is the organization's track record with female entrepreneurs?
- What are their most recent successes?
- Can they provide references?
- What are their most recent failures?
- How much experience do the contact people have in the "real world"?

Once the organization has been evaluated from the perspective of what they can give, they need to be evaluated in terms of what they expect. Most organizations charge some fee for membership or services, although governmental help givers such as the Small Business Development Centers do not. A woman business owner needs to be clear on any financial commitments as well as volunteer time that may be expected as a condition of membership or assistance.

FOCUSED INVOLVEMENT

The key to selecting help givers is clearly understanding what help is needed. Many women business owners spread themselves too thin by joining several organizations and seeking advice from a multitude of sources. If the woman is clear on her needs, she'll do a better job of choosing the organizations to work with. The maximum benefit from a help-giving organization comes from getting involved and forming deep rather than superficial relationships with the staff and volunteers. Good-quality relationships take time and energy to develop. The more a female entrepreneur is involved with a help-giving organization, the more she will receive in return.

NOTES

1. "Shaking the Venture Capital Tree," *New York Times*, March 11, 2001.

2. "Women Entrepreneurs in the Equity Capital Markets: The New Frontier," (Washington D.C.: National Foundation of Women Business Owners, 2000). Underwritten by Wells Fargo Bank.

3. "Fast-Growth Women and Men Entrepreneurs Take Different Paths Toward Business Success" (Washington, D.C.: National Foundation of Women Business Owners, 2001). Sponsored by the Edward Lowe Foundation, the Kauffman Center for Entrepreneurial Leadership and Fleet Boston Financial.

11

Entry-Strategy Analysis, Monitoring, and Evaluation of Programs in Support of Female Entrepreneurs

It isn't enough to make sure you're on the right track; you must also make sure you're not going in the wrong direction.

Anonymous

We know that women establish businesses for different reasons from men and they often start businesses in different markets and with different business structures. Therefore, programs that support and encourage female entrepreneurship need to directly address the needs of women business owners. For instance, women need better access to capital with programs that recognize the unique needs of women. Moreover, women often request smaller loans than men—a fact that often works against them.

Women business owners need to have the opportunity to learn how to compete effectively. This should include strategies to utilize technology, which enables them to capitalize on innovation. Women business owners gain tremendous advantage through organizations that encourage networking and partnerships, which give them a competitive advantage. Women can have greater access to markets by forming relationships with trade associations and large companies' procurement programs. And finally, by encouraging a favorable institutional and regulatory environment, women business owners will

be less burdened with the barriers of excessive taxation and reporting.[1]

Despite the billions of dollars spent each year on programs designed to empower women, still very little is known about the actual
impact of the projects. There is broad evidence on the benefits of
economic growth and investments in human capital, but for a specific
program in a specific region, the following questions are very often
quite difficult to answer:

• Did the project or program produce the intended benefits?
• What was the overall impact on the population?
• Could the program or project have been better designed to achieve the
  intended outcomes?
• Were the resources used efficiently?

These are the questions that can be answered only through an impact
evaluation, an approach that measures the outcomes of a program
intervention after excluding other possible factors.

It is disheartening, however, that too many governments, institutions, organizations, and project managers are reluctant to carry out
such necessary studies because they are seen as expensive, time con-
suming, and technically complex and because the findings can be po-
litically sensitive, particularly if they are negative. Often the data is
scarce and poor in quality besides. Many evaluations have also been
criticized because the results come too late, do not answer the right
questions, or were not carried out with sufficient analytical rigor.

Failing to accurately assess impact is particularly damaging in developing countries where resources are scarce and every dollar spent
must maximize its impact on poverty reduction. If programs are
poorly designed, do not reach their intended beneficiaries, or are
wasteful, with the right information they can be redesigned, improved, or eliminated if necessary. The knowledge gained from impact evaluation studies needs to provide critical input to the
appropriate design of future programs and projects.[2] If they are not
assessed properly, nothing can be done. Unfortunately, a large number of programs and projects come up short in providing all the desired benefits to the women they are seeking to empower.

Linked to the shortcomings of impact evaluations in many projects
in support of female entrepreneurs is the failure to establish an effective entry-analysis program. The scheme discussed here is intended
to provide donors, project managers, and policy analysts with the

tools to assess entry strategies and metrics for analyzing project effectiveness. In other words, it provides a clearer road map for those entities looking to maximize the effectiveness of their programs and projects.

SETTING GOALS AND TARGETS AND USING INDICATORS

The establishment of a coherent entry analysis, monitoring, and evaluation strategy in support of female entrepreneurs is centered on setting goals and targets by the supporting entity.

For our purposes, *goals* are defined as the objectives that a supporting entity wants to achieve. They may be expressed in nontechnical, terms, such as "eliminate female poverty" or "reduce incidences of AIDS in women." Agreeing on the goals in support of female entrepreneurs is a strong way to focus efforts and resources and help prioritize objectives. Setting clear goals can add a degree of clarity to the process of resource distribution and provides a benchmark against which to monitor the success of a program or project.

Measuring progress toward the accomplishment of goals is done through the creation of *indicators*. They are the variables used to measure progress toward the goals. For example, progress toward eliminating female poverty could be measured by looking at the number of women who are living under the poverty levels of their nation.[3]

Targets are the quantifiable levels of the indicators that a supporting entity wants to achieve at a given point in time—for example "the poverty rate of urban women in Ohio should be cut in half by 2005."

In the mid-1990s, the Organization for Economic Cooperation and Development (OECD), the United Nations, and the World Bank, in partnership with several developing countries, established explicit goals and targets to monitor progress in reducing world poverty. Known as the International Development Goals, they were categorized as follows:

For economic well-being:

• Reduce by half the proportion of people living in extreme poverty by 2015.

For social development:

• Achieve universal primary education in all countries by 2015.
• Eliminate gender disparities in primary and secondary education by 2005.

- Provide access to reproductive health services for all individuals of appropriate age no later than 2015.

For environmental regeneration:

- Reverse trends in the loss of environmental resources by 2015.

After setting the goals, the next step is to identify the indicators to measure progress toward those goals. Because one indicator can rarely reflect the extent to which a given goal has been achieved, several indicators can and should be used.[4] In the above example, at least one indicator was selected for each goal. For example, for the poverty reduction goal, the following indicators were used:

- Incidence of extreme poverty: below $1 per day
- Poverty gap ratio
- Poorest fifth's share of national consumption
- Percentage of underweight children under five

Indicators can be broadly classified into two groups: intermediate and final. When an indicator measures a factor that determines an outcome or contributes to the process of achieving an outcome, depending on the stage of the process—it is an *intermediate indicator*. For example, many things may be needed to raise literacy levels: more schools and teachers, more people attending classes, for example.

When an indicator measures a final goal or the effect of an intervention, it is a *final indicator*. With regard to the literacy example, the proportion of people of a certain age who can read a simple text and write their names would be a *final indicator*.

Both intermediate indicators and final indicators are important, but they serve very different and useful purposes. Intermediate indicators are most useful in tracking progress, or the lack thereof, over time. They give a more timely picture of what is happening. They can also help identify which of the several factors influencing an outcome is not on track and indicate what corrective action could be taken.

Final indicators help to judge progress toward the targets set. When complemented with other indicators, final indicators can help to measure overall performance and account for the context in which the measurement is taking place.[5]

Generally speaking, good indicators share a number of common characteristics:

- The indicator is a direct and unambiguous measure of progress.
- The indicator is relevant.
- The indicator varies across areas and groups over time and is sensitive to changes in policies, programs, and institutions.
- The indicator is not distracted by unrelated developments and cannot be easily manipulated to show success where none exists.
- The indicator can be tracked and is available frequently.

COLLECTING DATA

Data collection for entry-strategy analysis can be both costly and time-consuming. The main challenge for those seeking to support female entrepreneurs is how to take advantage of existing data sources and how to plan additional data collection to maximize its use for entry-strategy analysis.

Effective entry-strategy analyses draw on a variety of data sources. Therefore, one of the early steps in designing an entry strategy is to take stock of the types and quality of data already available. Moreover, many of the data used for entry analysis may also be quite useful for evaluating impact.

To be truly useful, the data used in entry-strategy analyses should be vertically integrated throughout the players in the project or program. For example, findings that emphasize implications for policy and program design should be distributed among government officials, donors, nongovernmental organizations, and other related agencies. Workshops and seminars should be organized to share results among local governments and civil organizations.

Further, findings and recommendations must be accessible to community councils, local women's organizations, and other groups representing communities to whom programs are targeted. Most of these groups, especially in the developing world, may not have access to information technology and conventional dissemination mechanisms. In these cases, alternative dissemination methods such as posters, pamphlets, and meetings might be needed.

THE INTEGRATIVE APPROACH

There is a need to integrate the various approaches and indicators to program entry strategy, monitoring, and evaluation. For example, survey data from statistically representative samples may be better suited to assessing causality. Qualitative and participatory methods play their role by enabling the in-depth study of selected issues, cases, or events and can provide critical insights into beneficiaries' perspectives, the dynamics of a particular reform, or the reasons behind certain results observed in a quantitative analysis.[6]

Integrating quantitative, qualitative, and participatory indicators can often be the best vehicle for meeting the program's entry strategy, monitoring, and evaluation needs. For example, qualitative methods can be used to inform the evaluation questions and the questionnaire design, as well as to analyze the social, economic, and political context within which a program or policy takes place. Similarly, quantitative methods can be used to inform qualitative data-collection strategies, including sample design. Statistical analysis controlling for household characteristics and the socioeconomic conditions of different study areas serves to eliminate alternative explanations of the outcomes observed in qualitative studies. A number of benefits arise from integrated approaches in entry-strategy analysis, monitoring, and evaluation.

Consistency checks can be built in through triangulation via independent estimates for key variables (such as income, opinions about projects, reasons for using or not using public services, and specific impact of a project).

Different *perspectives* can be obtained. For example, although researchers may consider income or consumption to be the key indicators of household welfare, case studies may reveal that women are more concerned about vulnerability (defined as the lack of access to social support systems in times of crisis), powerlessness, or exposure to violence.

Analysis can be conducted on different *levels*. Survey methods can provide good estimates of individual, household, and community-level welfare, but they are much less effective for analyzing social processes (social conflict, reasons for using or not using services, and so on) or for institutional analysis (how effectively health, education, credit, and other services operate and how they are perceived by the community). There are many qualitative methods designed to analyze issues such as social process, institutional behavior, social structure, and conflict.

Opportunities can be provided for *feedback* to help interpret findings. Survey reports frequently include references to apparent inconsistencies in findings or to interesting differences between communities or groups that cannot be explained by the data. In most quantitative research, once the data collection phase is completed it is not possible to return to the field to check on such questions. In many cases the data analyst has to make an arbitrary decision whether to exclude a household or community that significantly deviates from the norm (on the assumption that it reflects a reporting error) or whether to adjust the figures. The greater flexibility of qualitative research means that it is often possible to return to the field to gather additional data, which allows a rapid follow-up for deviant cases.

Good quality information is essential for the design of sound, appropriate policies. It is not an easy task to determine the number of women entrepreneurs from official statistics in either developed or developing countries. The figures are often incomplete or based on sample analyses. There is no unique formal definition of what constitutes a female enterprise since no clear analytical threshold for this concept exists. For example, firms are sometimes classified according to their turnover, number of employees, or legal status. Statistics regarding women are even more problematic as most surveys do not take gender into account.

This situation is partly due to historical factors or civil liberties that prohibit the collection and publication of certain information by national statistical systems. Detailed statistics concerning income and wealth are therefore particularly difficult to obtain from some countries. The organization of data collection at an international level poses further problems, both in terms of access and coherence for comparative purposes.

DESIGNING ENTRY-ANALYSIS STRATEGY, MONITORING, AND EVALUATION

Designing an evaluating strategy involves deciding what policies and programs should be evaluated, defining the expected outcomes and when they will be measured, selecting an evaluation, and obtaining the data needed.

Figure 11.1 displays a twelve-part scheme of metrics for entry-analysis, monitoring, and evaluation strategies in support of female entrepreneurs. Each metric is categorized into one of four areas: programs, policies, climate, and competitiveness.

Figure 11.1
Twelve-Part Scheme for Evaluating the Environment for Female Entrepreneurship

Programs	Policies
•Women's Level of Education and Training	•Women's Participation in Economic Activities
•Existing Programs That Support Women Entrepreneurs	•Economic and Political Analysis
•Involvement of Female Entrepreneurs in the Programs Designed for Them	•Level of Feminization of Poverty
Climate	**Competitiveness**
•Public Perception of Female Entrepreneurs	•Adoption of Technology by Female Entrepeneurs
•Participation and Support by the Private Sector	•Women's Access to Credit
•Impact of Globalization	•Strategic Investment by Female Entrepreneurs

Programs

Women's Level of Education and Training

Professional and lifestyle choices are strongly influenced by social-ization processes, in which schooling plays an important role. Uni-versal schooling is unquestionably a powerful tool for promoting equal opportunity. At the same time, however, schools have a natural tendency to replicate existing social structures, including sexual ster-eotypes. Thus, while girls are increasingly attaining a level of edu-cation equivalent or superior to that of boys, the teaching that they receive, or choose to receive, differs from that of boys in significant ways. This is particularly true of training related to professional life.

Developed countries today seem to attach an increasing importance to the interrelationship between education and the economy. Edu-cation can take a narrow or a broad approach to what enterprise means and the practice of it. The narrow approach is directly business-oriented, teaching, for example, what is required for business startup and management. The narrow approach calls for curriculum development and experiential learning. The broad approach focuses on personal development, on qualities and competencies that enable people to be flexible, creative, and adaptable. It requires changes in educational methods and pedagogy.

Approaches based on the narrow definition have developed significantly, mainly promoted by the private sector and directed at the elite. More recently governments have adopted policies and programs to promote and assist entrepreneurship targeted at the unemployed.

Policy and practice derived from the broad approach are still at an experimental stage, and nowhere have they progressed from the innovative fringe into the mainstream. They are often seen as an innovative learning technique for the less able. Current practices thus reveal that enterprise is not seen as relevant to everyone.

Education faces two challenges for its role in attracting and preparing more girls to be enterprising. These challenges will need to be pursued concurrently unless the situation changes in a fundamental way:

- How can girls' participation in business preparation programs at all levels of the educational system (secondary and postsecondary) be increased?
- What is needed for schools at all levels to adopt methods focusing on personal development for all?

Existing Programs That Support Women Entrepreneurs

The associations that women have formed to access markets provide support, mentoring, training, and catalyst opportunities for women entrepreneurs to begin building networks with government procurement officials and corporate buyers. Policy and decision makers may wish to consider:

- How can governments remove legal and regulatory barriers to women's entrepreneurship?
- How can governments foster a conducive regulatory environment, including taxation systems?
- What steps can government and international institutions take to strengthen associations of women entrepreneurs?
- What role can multinational corporations play in this process?

Involvement of Female Entrepreneurs in the Programs Designed for Them

The question here is, are women playing an active role? This essentially takes a look from a bottom-up approach. In too many instances, programs and policies in support of female entrepreneurship have been designed and implemented that failed to take into account the invaluable perspectives and contributions of the women they were trying to support. The end result is a failure to maximize the efficacy of the policy or program. Women must be involved in the process. Their involvement also provides a means to evaluate the environment for female entrepreneurship in their region.

Policies

Women's Participation in Economic Activities

SMEs frequently complain about the imposition of regulations and administrative burdens upon their operations. The complaint is the disproportionate amount of time (and hence costs) a small firm must spend on such administrative matters, compared with larger firms, which are able to defray the cost over a larger revenue base and the labor over a larger staff.

For women, the regulation and administrative burdens are even heavier both because they tend to set up SMEs and because they may have less experience in acquiring information on the relevant administrative regulations and in carrying out many administrative formalities. In addition to these burdens—which affect all SMEs—women entrepreneurs sometimes face difficulties because of their legal status. Indeed, the choice of a legal structure for a business is a vital factor that may effect levels of taxation, profitability, social security, and retirement benefits. In this context, female co-entrepreneurs are often dependent on their partners for these social benefits, and in many countries the fiscal system is often not adapted to their status as women co-entrepreneurs. Therefore, the acknowledgment of their role and rights in relation to other family members in a family-owned business is a crucial issue.

Removing regulatory obstacles can contribute to a conducive business environment for SMEs, and particularly for woman-owned SMEs. In addition, however, there is a need for effective support structures for woman-owned businesses.

Economic and Political Analysis

Several environmental factors in a region must be part of a relevant analysis:

- Macroeconomic stability
- Inflation rate
- Increasing GDP
- Increasing savings
- Political stability
- Government bureaucracy and regulations
- Incentives for doing business with women

Level of Feminization of Poverty

- A prevalence of women among the poor
- Structural causes of gender bias in the impact of poverty
- A directional trend of increasingly disproportionate representation of women among the poor
- The visibility of female poverty

Climate

Public Perception of Female Entrepreneurs

In spite of recent improvements, women business owners have not received the attention they deserve from national and local authorities, educational institutions, from the world of business and finance, or the media. An analysis of television, radio, newspaper, and Internet structures should be undertaken.

Participation and Support by the Private Sector

The problem of access is also apparent in outsourcing contracts of large companies. While large corporations may have aggressive business partner, supplier, and outsourcing programs, because women entrepreneurs often are not part of influential, primarily male, business networks, they often find themselves excluded from corporate business opportunities.

This may also be the case for second-tier and third-tier subcontracting programs developed by large multinational corporations, which have encouraged SME suppliers of goods and services to begin exporting. For example, if a prime contractor has sold equipment to a firm in Thailand, a second-tier exporter might provide replacement parts and the third-tier exporter might provide training in the effective use of the equipment.

Impact of Globalization

As chapter 2 described, globalization is one of the most important aspects of our lives today. How female entrepreneurs respond to the global economy is one of their greatest challenges. They especially need to analyze the specific effects of globalization where they plan to do business.

Although the flexibility of SMEs give them advantages in adjusting to market evolution, access to markets remains problematic in a competitive environment that does not always work to their advantage. Access can be particularly difficult for public procurement and subcontracting, for one example. Besides, many internationalized SMEs face trade and investment barriers, particularly in developing countries, such as tariff barriers and customs regulations. Developing countries may limit market access intentionally or unintentionally by such mechanisms as approval procedures, the fees for establishing a legal standing, the difficulties in creating local partnerships (such as alliances of franchises), or cultural impediments to distribution channels or resources.

All SMEs face challenges in accessing foreign markets: inadequate market intelligence, inadequate access to capital, and inadequate knowledge of international trade laws and regulations. Woman-owned SMEs can find those challenges especially daunting.

The two primary international groups of women entrepreneurs are Les Femmes Chefs d'Entreprises Mondiales (FCEM), a thirty-four-country group headquartered in the Netherlands, and the International Federation of Women Entrepreneurs, headquartered in New Delhi. Thousands of primarily local groups of women entrepreneurs exist in countries around the world. These networks, through personal contacts and the sharing of know-how, open up important avenues for women entrepreneurs.

Competitiveness

Adoption of Technology by Female Entrepreneurs

Technology and the information revolution are thoroughly changing the way small firms do business. Technology plays an increasingly important role in all aspects of competitiveness: products and production techniques, as well as management methods, firm organization, and staff training.

Because of new technologies, the small manufacturer or producer, whether a women's cooperative or a lone woman in a home-based business, has greater production capability as well as access to markets today than could only be imagined just a few years ago. To benefit from these new technologies, women entrepreneurs should first know the basics of running a business (e.g., creating and revisiting a business plan) and solving the daily problems of staying in business. Women entrepreneurs are often less prepared and have different business backgrounds than their male counterparts. Like most SME owners, they also have difficulties accessing the scientific, technological, and economic information that is of vital importance to stay competitive.

SMEs in general face a number of constraints in this regard: lack of time, experience, and skilled specialist staff for sorting through the mass of information available on the market. Business training is essential in this regard, but an assimilation into the technological culture is the only way to stay current and capitalize on the technological possibilities as they arise. Since every SME and every technology's culture is different, no general statement is possible. This is a business social skill than can be learned only by doing.

Women's Access to Credit

The woman entrepreneur must assess the financial and credit environment in her area of operation. This involves the analysis of two factors: the constraints to women's participation in the credit system and the differences between formal and informal credit methods.

The following self-assessment will provide a better understanding of the barriers to women's access to credit mechanisms.

- Illiteracy/low level of education
- Class/family restrictions
- Inaccessible localities
- Ignorance about credit facilities
- Ignorance about business (profit/loss)
- Low economic status of the family
- Heavy burden of children/household work
- Frequency of childbearing

- Routine responsibilities for family care and services
- Male domination in dealings outside the home

Survey formal credit institutions—banks and government—and informal credit ones—NGOs and private firms, on the following criteria. Categories such as "none, inadequate, adequate, strong" or "none, negligible, detailed, complex" could be used. The results will suggest the most viable opportunities.

- Awareness of service relations with borrowers
- Procedures for membership
- Eligibility criteria
- Relevance to needs of borrowers
- Lending procedures and documentation
- Frequency of loans
- Repayment rates
- Savings
- Noncredit inputs
- Size of loans

Most SME owners or future owners are in the position of having to borrow in order both to set up and develop their companies. Most frequently, creditors have imperfect information about the quality or intentions of those who wish to borrow. To develop a sense of trust that the debtor is a sound investment, the creditor requires information about the debtor. Information gathering requires the creditor to expend a sunk, fixed cost in that effort, which will be bigger the more information the creditor has to gather about the debtor or the more alien the debtor's experience or approach to management is, for example.

The majority of women establish very small enterprises in the service and retail sectors, which represent the less expanded sectors and which operate most of the time in local markets. In addition, in many countries, the enterprises operating in the sector of commerce tend to have a much lower survival rate. Women have entered the labor market later than men, within a limited range of professions, and are therefore often less experienced professionally than men, particularly in management and supervision.

Women typically apply for smaller loans, which to a banker resemble a personal loan, and which they tend to approach from that point of view. Underestimation of financial requirements in relation to the enterprise they are establishing, or reluctance to borrow larger sums, can adversely affect the perceptions of banks and organizations regarding the viability of a woman's firm.

Self-employed women, or women business owners operating under specific juridical statutes, are often reluctant to use family assets as collateral, and in some cases must obtain their husbands' agreement to obtain loans.

Despite the growing number of small enterprises and their important economic role, investors have been less inclined to invest in many of these firms because of the perceived cost difficulties of evaluating them. In their effort to modernize and become more competitive, banks often focus on servicing large and medium-sized companies to the detriment of small enterprises. Policy and decision makers may wish to consider

- How to deepen the knowledge of financing of woman-owned SMEs, particularly very small enterprises (e.g., the average size of loans, the percentage of loan applications that are successful, the percentage of failed loans, the impact of partnership agreements between intermediary organizations and banks.)
- How "good practices" related to the financing of small enterprises can be identified, assessed and disseminated with an aim to promote financial products and tools that have proven effective
- The role and best form of public-private partnerships to encourage more investment in woman-owned SMEs.

Strategic Investment by Female Entrepreneurs

The competitiveness of female entrepreneurs depends on strategies and renewed tangible and intangible investment. Tangible investment refers to expenditures or efforts to acquire technologically suitable equipment. Intangible investment includes a capacity for research and development and an ability to ally with research institutions; staff training; the quality of business organization; the ability to obtain, and use efficiently, information on technological, commercial, and competitive developments; and the ability to use software effectively.

Investment is not sufficient in itself if small businesses are not also able to display strategic capabilities. In particular, they must display flexibility to seize market opportunities and adjust rapidly to changes in demand and innovation, which is the most crucial factor in competition. Indeed, firms are learning to "shift their priorities from sta-bilizing to innovating." Enterprises must continually reinvent themselves, and organizational innovations can be even more impor-tant than product technology and market innovations.

Competitive strategies vary widely with the type of SME, sector, location, market development, regulatory framework, and economic situation.

The decision on frequency of monitoring, like those on indicators of the integration approach, depends on a careful assessment of the tradeoff between the desirability for good data and the cost of col-lection.

PROMOTING PARTICIPATION IN ENTRY STRATEGY, MONITORING, AND EVALUATION

Broad-based participation in entry-strategy analysis, monitoring, and evaluation is critical to creating a sense of ownership amongst the stakeholders of a program in support of female entrepreneurs. If properly done, the acceptance and use of the finding is increased. Moreover, consensus among stakeholders enhances the monitoring and evaluation efforts by creating agreement on what outcomes to monitor and what impacts to evaluate. Consensus building also allows the incorporation of individuals' perceptions of their well-being as a critical outcome to be monitored.

Participation in entry-strategy analysis, monitoring, and evaluation can be promoted in four areas:

Goal setting: Consensus around goals and objectives can be built through consultations with women and with different sectors, includ-ing government agencies, organized local groups, and the private sec-tor. This in turn can build support for the overall strategy to increase the number of female entrepreneurs.

Encouraging qualitative methodologies: The use of qualitative methods to complement qualitative approaches for entry-strategy analysis, monitoring, and evaluation can foster participation. Qualitative meth-ods usually involve local people, allowing them to have a voice in decisions on resource allocation, priority areas of intervention, and service delivery.

Collaboration in data collection and analysis: Participation can also be promoted by involving groups and organizations in data collection and analysis, including academics, NGOs, and local governments.

This can be most useful in building an in-country infrastructure for monitoring and evaluating.

Dissemination of findings: Wide dissemination of results encourages participation. By ensuring that stakeholders have access to entry-strategy analysis, monitoring, and evaluation findings, it is possible to generate a participatory review process of female entrepreneurs that increases accountability and transparency of pubic resource allocation and public actions.

NOTES

1. Judy Baker, *Evaluating the Impact of Development Projects on Poverty: A Handbook for Practitioners* (Washington, D.C.: World Bank, 2000).

2. Ibid.

3. Ibid.

4. Ibid.

5. Ibid.

6. Ibid.

Afterword

The tremendous growth in female entrepreneurs across the globe is an exciting phenomenon. It inspires in many of us a desire to understand why such an unprecedented number of women are starting businesses. In this book, we have attempted to document and identify this trend, not just in the United States, but in other developed and developing countries throughout the world.

We've also sought to present an understanding of why this trend is taking place. The move toward a global economy, the growth in technology, and the opening of economies has affected the trend from a macroeconomic level. On a microeconomic level, the changing nature of family, the increasing educational level of women, the change in societal attitudes toward women working, and women's own desire for personal satisfaction are driving this trend.

In an effort to assist female entrepreneurs, we have also discussed how to give them help. By understanding the unique challenges that female entrepreneurs face, organizations can tailor their programs to assist women as they start and grow their enterprises.

We have attempted to include research from a variety of sources throughout the world that help us to understand this trend. Thankfully governmental and nongovernmental organizations recognize the need to further research and understand this topic. Accurate detailed research on women business owners is still lacking, however, especially in the developing world.

We welcome comments, ideas, and suggestions on this topic. You can contact us at The Coughlin Group, Inc., e-mail: info@ cgroupinc.com.

Appendix I: Female Entrepreneurship Resource Guide

In the following pages, we have put together a set of basic contact information for several countries with regard to research, support, consulting, and fostering of female entrepreneurs. While we have done our best to include the very latest and most complete information, we cannot guarantee that some details will not have changed by or after publication. Inclusion of foreign, private, or non-governmental organizations in this directory do not suggest their endorsement.

ALBANIA

Women's Center
P.O. Box 2418
Tirana, Albania
E-mail: postmaster@women-center.tirana.al

ARGENTINA

Center for the Study of Women
Avenida Santa Fe 5380, 70 E
(1425) Buenos Aires, Argentina
E-mail: cem@cembue.wamani.apc.org

Centro de Estudios de Estado y Sociedad
Hipolito Yrigoyen 1156
(1086) Buenos Aires, Argentina

Centro de Estudios de Población (CENEP)
Corrientes 2817, Piso 7
(1193) Buenos Aires, Argentina
E-mail: system@cenep.satlink.net

GT Condición Femenina Clasco
(Latin American Council of Social Sciences)
Avenida Pueyrredon 510–70
(1032) Buenos Aires, Argentina

Equipo de Envestigación Asistencia para la Mujer
Beruti 3032
(1425) Buenos Aires, Argentina

Fundación Alicia Moreau de Justo
Corrientes 1485, 19 "A"
(1042) Buenos Aires, Argentina

Instituto Social y Político de la Mujer
Avenida Callao 741, 1° Piso
(1030) Buenos Aires, Argentina

Participación Social para Mujeres Argentinas
(Argentine Women's Social Participation)
Dorrego 2373
(1425) Buenos Aires, Argentina

ARMENIA

Armenia Center for Alternative Education and the Arts
23 Bagramian Street, Suite 23
Yerevan, Armenia

AUSTRALIA

Office of the Status of Women
Department of the Prime Minister and Cabinet
3–5 National Circuit
Barton, Australia 2600
E-mail: women@dpmc.gov.au
Web site: www.dpmc.gov.au

Research Center for Gender Studies
University of South Australia
St. Bernards Road
South Australia
Magill, Australia 5072

Research Center for Women's Studies
University of Adelaide
G.P.O. Box 498
South Australia
Adelaide, Australia 5005

Australian Women's Research Center
Deakin University
Pigdon's Road
Victoria
Geelon, Australia 3217
E-mail: aworc@deakin.edu.au
Web site: www2.deakin.edu.au

Institute for Women's Studies
Macquarie University
N.S.W., Australia 2019

Australian Institute for Women's Research and Policy
Griffith University
Queensland, Australia 4111

Women's Research Unit
The University of Sydney
127 Darlington Road
N.S.W.
Sydney, Australia 2006

AUSTRIA

Dokumentation Frauenforschung
Institut fur Wissenschaft und Kunst
1090 Wien
Berggasse 17/1
Vienna, Austria 1090

BANGLADESH

Foundation for Research on Educational Planning and Development
(FREDPD)

64/A Green Road
Dhaka—1205—Bangladesh

International Women Studies Institute
71 Satmasjid Road
Dhanmandi R.A.
Dhaka—Bangladesh

Institute for Development Studies
E-17 Agargaon
Sher-e-Bangla Nagar
Dhaka—7—Bangladesh

Women for Women
15 Green Square
Green Road
Dhaka—1205—Bangladesh

BARBADOS

The Bureau of Women's Affairs
Ministry of Labor and Community Development
Fairchild Street
Bridgetown, Barbados

Caribbean Policy Development Center (CPDC)
GPO Box 284
Welches Road
St. Michael, Barbados
E-mail: cpdc@caribnet.net

Center for Gender and Development Studies (CGDS)
University of the West Indies
P.O. Box 284
Bridgetown, Barbados

BELARUS

Center for Gender Studies
European Humanities University
24 pr. Skirony
Minsk—220030—Belarus
E-mail: gender@ehu.unibel.by

BELGIUM

Center for Research on European Women (CREW)
38 Rue Stevin
(1040) Brussels, Belgium

Center for Women's Studies
University of Gent
Baertsoenkaai 3
(9000) Gent, Belgium

BOLIVIA

Centro de Información y Desarrollo de la Mujer
22433, Av. Villazon, of. 3A
La Paz, Bolivia

BRAZIL

Carlos Chagas Foundation
Avenue Professor Francisco Morato, 1565
Caixa Postal 11478
São Paulo 05513, Brazil

Center for the Study of Women and Gender (NEMGE)
Nucleo de Estudo da Mulher e Relacões Sociais de Genero
University of São Paulo
Antiga Reitoria Sala 310
Cidade Universitaria
São Paulo SP 05508–900, Brazil
E-mail: eblay@usp.br

Centro Feminista de Estudios e Assessoria (CFEMEA)
Feminist Center for Studies and Advice
SCN Quadra 6—Ed. Venancio 3000 Bl.A Sala 602
CEP 70718–900 Brasilia-DF, Brazil

Centro Informação Mulher (CIM)
R. Fernão Dias 128/Apt. 92A
São Paulo, Brazil

Instituto de Estudios Economia, Politica, y Sociologia
Av. Dr. Arnaldo, 1973
Sumare, São Paulo, CEP 01255, Brazil

Instituto Universitario de Pesquisas de Rio de Janeiro
Rua Paulino Fernandes, 32
Rio de Janeiro 22270, Brazil

Women's Studies Center
Pontifical Catholic University
Rua Marques São Vincente 225
Rio de Janeiro 22453, Brazil

BULGARIA

Women's Studies Centre
New Bulgarian University
P.O. Box 135
Sofia—1618, Bulgaria

CANADA

Canadian Research Institute for the Advancement of Women (CRIAW)
415–151 Slater, Suite 408
Ottawa, ON K1P 5H3, Canada
E-mail: criaw@sympatico.ca
Web site: www.criaw-icref.ca

McGill Centre for Research and Teaching on Women
McGill University
3487 Peel Street, Second Floor
Montreal, PQ H3A 1W7, Canada

Simone de Beauvoir Institute
Concordia University
1455 de Maissoneuve Boulevard West
Montreal, PQ H3G 1M8, Canada
E-mail: ssull@vax2.concordia.ca

Institute for the Study of Women
Mount Saint Vincent University
166 Bedford Highway
Halifax, NS B3M 2J6, Canada
E-mail: judy.mccluskey@msva.ca
Web site: www.msvu.ca

Centre for Women's Studies in Education
Ontario Institute for Studies in Education
252 Bloor Street West, Rm S630
Toronto, ON M5S 1V6, Canada

Women's Studies Research Unit
University of Saskatchewan
Education Building
Saskatoon SK S7N 0W0, Canada

Feminist Institute for Studies on Law and Society
Simon Fraser University
Burnaby, BC V5A 1S6, Canada

Women and Environments
Centre for Urban and Community Studies
455 Spadina Avenue, Room 426
Toronto, ON M5S 2G8, Canada

Center for Research in Women's Studies and Gender Relations
1896 East Mall
University of British Columbia
Vancouver, BC V6T 1Z1, Canada
E-mail: joey@unixg.ubc.ca
Web site: www.wmst.ubc.ca

Centre for Women's Studies and Feminist Research
University of Western Ontario
University College 124
London, ON N6A 3K7, Canada
E-mail: jashford@julian.uwo.ca
Web site: www.uwo.ca/womens/index.html

York Center for Feminist Research
Le Centre de recherche feminist à York
York University
228 York Lanes, 4700 Keele Street
North York, ON M3J 1P3, Canada

CHILE

Centro de Estudios de la Mujer
(Center for Women's Studies)
Purísima 353, Santiago, Chile
Web site: www.argumentos.cem.cl

Domos (Centre de Desarrollo para la Mujer)
Los Lilenes 130
La Florida, Santiago, Chile

Facultad Latinoamericana de Ciencias Sociales
FLACSO Chile
Leopoldo Urrutia 1950, Ñuñoa
Santiago, Chile
E-mail: agenero@flacso.cl

CHINA

The Women's Studies and Information Center
Chinese Women's College
No. 1 Yuhui Donglu, Chaoyang District
Beijing 100101, China

Women's Studies Center, Population Institute
Fudan University
Shanghai 200433, China

Center for Women's Studies
Shaanxi Teachers University
P.O. Box 45
Xian 710062, China

Women's Studies Center
Beijing Foreign Studies University
P.O. Box 8110
Beijing 100081, China

Study Center for Women in Social Development of China
Heber Social Sciences Academy
No. 9 Shi Yi Road
Shijiazhuang, Hebei, China

Women's Research Institute
All China Women's Federation
No. 50 Dengskikou Street
Beijing 100730, China

Women's Studies Center
Faculty of Social Sciences
Hainan University
Haikou, 570228, China
E-mail: lipin@mail.hainu.edu.cn

Center for Women's Studies
Department of English
Peking University
Beijing, 100781, China

Women's Studies Center
Chinese Department
Zhengzhou University
Zhenzhou City, Henan Province, China

Marriage and Family Research Center
Anhui University
Hefei, Anhui, China

Women's Studies Center
Party School of the Central Committee of the C.P.C.
100 Dayouzhuang, Haidian District
Beijing, China

COLOMBIA

Center of Economic Development Studies (CEDE)
University of Los Andes
Apartado Aereo 4976
Bogota, Colombia

COSTA RICA

ASESORA
Centro Nacional para el Desarrollo de la Mujer y la Familia
(National Center for the Development of Women and the Family)
Ministerio de Cultura, Juventud y Deporte
Apartado 10.227–1000
San José, Costa Rica

Programa de Información para la Mujer
Universidad Nacional
Apartado 86–3000
Heredia, Costa Rica

Programa Interdisciplinario de Estudios de Genero
Universidad de Costa Rica
San José, Costa Rica

CROATIA

Be Active Be Emancipated (B.a.B.e.)
Women's Human Rights Group
Prilaz Gjure Dezelica 26/II
10 000 Zagreb, Croatia
E-mail: babe_zg@zamir-zg.ztn.apc.org
Web site: www.interlog.com/~moyra

Center for Women's Studies
Berislaviaeva 12/I (c/o) Goluza
10 000 Zagreb, Croatia
E-mail: zenstud@zamir.net
Web site: www.zamir.net/~zenstud

Women's Information and Documentation Center in Croatia
Varsavska 16
10000 Zagreb, Croatia
E-mail: zinfo@zamir.net
Web site: www.zamir.net

CZECH REPUBLIC

East–West Gender Studies
P.O. Box 188
CS—1121 Praha, Czech Republic

Centrum pro Gender Studies
Narodni dum Smichov
Nam. 14 Rijna 16
150 00 Praha 5, Czech Republic
E-mail: gender@ecn.cz
Web site: www.ecn.cz/gender

DENMARK

CEKVINA (Women's Research Center in Aarhus)
University of Aarhus
Finlandsgade 26
DK-8200, Aarhus N, Denmark

Center for Feminist Research and Women's Studies
University of Copenhagen-Amager
Njalsgade 106
DK-2300 Copenhagen S, Denmark

Department for Feminist Research and Women's Studies
University of Southern Denmark
Odense University
Campusvej 55
DK-5230 Odense M, Denmark
E-mail: bro@litcul.sdu.dk
Web site: www.ou.dk/hum/studier/kstudier/kvindestudier.html

FREIA
Feminist Research Centre in Aalborg
Department of Development and Planning
Aalborg University
DK-9220 Aalborg, Denmark
E-mail: ravn@i4.auc.dk
Web site: www.i4.auc.dk/freia

KVINFO
Center for Information Omkviwoe-Og Kows Forskning
(The Danish Center for Information on Women and Gender)
Christians Brygge 3
Copenhagen 1219, Denmark
E-mail: kvinfo@inet.uni-c.dk
Web site: www.kulturnet.dk/homes/kvinfo

Women on the Edge
The Interdisciplinary Feminist Study and Research Center
History and Internationalization
Roskilde University
P.O. Box 260
DK-4000 Roskilde, Denmark
E-mail: kasj@ruc.dk

DOMINICAN REPUBLIC

Centro de Investigación para la Acción Femenina (CIPAF)
(Center for Research on Women's Action)
Calle Luis F. Thomen
358 Ensanche Quisqueya, Dominican Republic

Programa de Estudios de la Mujer
(Program for the Study of Women)
EQUIS-INTEC
Apartado Postal 156–9
Santo Domingo, Dominican Republic

UN International Research and Training Institute for the Advancement of
Women (INSTRAW)

102 A Avenida Cesar Nicolas Penson
Santo Domingo, Dominican Republic

ECUADOR

Instituto Ecuatoriano de Investigaciónes y Capacitación de la Mujer (IEC-AIM)
Avenida 6 de Diciembre 2817 y República
Quito, Ecuador

Centro de Planificatión y Estudios Sociales (CPPLAES)
Casilla 17–11–6127
Quito, Ecuador

Coordinadora de la Coalición Política de Mujeres Andinas
Lérida 493 y Toledo Sector La Floresta
Quito, Ecuador
E-mail: cd@ceplae.ecuanex.net.ec

EGYPT

Center for Egyptian Civilization Studies
18, Saray el Guezireh, Apt. 7
Cairo Zamalek, Egypt

New Woman Research Center
8 Wizaret El Zira's Street, Dokk 1
Cairo, Egypt

ESTONIA

Unit of Gender Studies
University of Tartu
78–231 Tiigi Street
EE-2400
Tartu, Estonia
E-mail: urmas@psych.ut.ee
Web site: www.@psych.ut.ee

Women's Studies Center
Tallinn Pedagogical University
Narva Rd.27
EE-0100
Tallinn, Estonia

E-mail: wstudies@tpu.ee
Web site: www.tpu.ee

ETHIOPIA

African Training and Research Center for Women
Box 3001
Addis Ababa, Ethiopia

Center for Research Training and Information for Women in Development
Addis Ababa University
P.O. Box 1176
Addis Ababa, Ethiopia

FINLAND

Institute for Women's Studies
Fin-20 500
Turku, Finland
E-mail: kvinnoforsk@abo.fi
Web site: www.abo.fi/instut/kvinnis/ifkvhems.htm

Center for Women's Studies and Gender Research
University of Tampere
P.O. Box 607
FIN-33101
Tampere, Finland
E-mail: nty@uta.fi
Web site: www.uta.fi/laitokset.naistukimus

FRANCE

Association pour le Dévelopment des Initiatives Economiques par les Femmes
1, allee des Rives de Bagatelle (ADIEF)
92150 Suresnes
France
Web site: www.swwb.org

CEDREF (Centre d'Enseignement de Documentation, de Recherche et d'Etudes Féministes)
Université de Paris VII Jussieu
2 place Jussieu
Couloir 24/34, 1er étage

Case postale 7132
75005 Paris, France

GEDISST (Research Group on the Social and Gender Division of Labor)
59–61 Rue Pouchet
Case Postale 17
75849 Paris, France

The World Association of Women Entrepreneurs (FCEM)
Lm. Yasmine App 1.1
Les Berges du lac. 1053 Tunis
Tunisie France
Web site: www.fcem.org
Email: wpresd.fcem@planet.tn

GEORGIA

Women's Studies Center
Tbilisi State University
Chavchavadze Ave 1
Tbilisi 380028, Georgia
E-mail: archilg@access.sanet.ge

GERMANY

Association of Business and Professional Women-Germany
Rothschildallee 55
60389 Frankfurt
Web site: www.bpw-germany.de
Monbecht@t-online.de

German Association of Women Entrepreneurs (VDU)
Breite Strasse 29
10178 Berlin
Web site: www.vdu.de
Email: info@vdu.de

University Center for the Promotion of Women's Studies
Free University of Berlin
Königin-Luise Strasse 34
D-14195 Berlin, Germany
E-mail: zefrauenazed@fu-berlin.de

Woman's Business Club Munich (Das Netzwerk Fur Businessfrauen Munich)
Franz-Prüller-Str. 15

81669 München
Web site: www.womans.de
Email: info@womans.de

Zentrum Interdisziplinaire Frauenforschung (ZIF)
Humbolt University
Sophienstrasse 22a
Unter den Linden 6
10099 Berlin, Germany
E-mail: zif@rx.hu-berlin.de
Web site: www.rz.hu-berlin.de

GHANA

Center for Women's Studies and Research
Legon University
North Accra, Ghana

GREECE

Mediterranean Women's Studies Unit (KEGME)
115, Harilaou Trikoupi Str.
114 73 Athens, Greece

GUYANA

Women's Study Unit
Faculty of Social Sciences
University of Guyana
P.O. Box 101110
Georgetown, Guyana

HONG KONG

Association for the Advancement of Feminism
G/F, 119–120, Lai Yeung House
Lei Cheng Uk Estate, Cheung Sha Wan
Kowloon, Hong Kong
E-mail: aaf@hk.super.net

HUNGARY

Women's Studies Center
Budapest University of Economic Sciences

Fouam Ter 8
Budapest, 1093, Hungary
E-mail: wsk_kk@pegasus.bke.hu

ICELAND

Center for Women's Studoes
Haskola Islands/University of Iceland
Oddi
15–101 Reykjavik, Iceland

INDIA

Anveshi Research Center for Women's Studies
Osmania University Campus
Hyberbad—500007—India

India Association for Women's Studies and Development
10–3–96 Plot 238, 4th Floor
Street 6, Teacher's Colony
East Marredpalli
Secunderabad—500026—India
E-mail: asmita@hdl.vsnl.net.in

Mother Teresa Women's University
13 Race Course Road
Guindy
Madras—600032—India

INDONESIA

Center for Women's Studies
University of North Sumatra
J1. Picauly, 14
Kampus USU
Medan, Indonesia

IRAN

Center for Women's Studies
P.O. Box 13145–654
Tehran, Iran

IRELAND

Women's Education, Research, and Resource Center
University College, Dublin
Room F 104B, Arts Building, UCD Belfield
Dublin, 4, Ireland
E-mail: werrc@ollamh.ucd.ie
Web site: www.ucd.ie/-werrc

ISRAEL

Center for Women's Studies
University of Haifa
Mount Carmel, Israel

ITALY

Pari e Dispari
Via Pacini, 22
Milano, 20131, Italy

JAMAICA

Center for Gender and Development Studies
University of the West Indies
Mona Campus
Kingston 7, Jamaica

JAPAN

International Center for Social Development (IRCSD)
14–1, 3 Chome, Shime Ochiai
Shinjuku-ku
Tokyo, 161, Japan

National Women's Education Center (NWEC)
Kokuritsu Fujin Kyoiku Kaikan
728 Sugaya
Hiki-gun, Razan-machi 728
Saitama Prefecture, 355–02, Japan
E-mail: webmaster@nwec.go.jp
Web site: www.nwec.go.jp

KENYA

Gender and Development Center
P.O. Box 1588
Kisumu, Kenya

KOREA

Korean Women's Development Institute
1–363 Bulkwang-dong
Eunpyung-ku
Seoul, 122–070, Korea
E-mail: sunny@kwominet.or.kr
Web site: www.kwominet.or.kr

Korean Women's Development Institute
Lifelong Education and International Cooperation Divisions
Seoul, Korea
E-mail: soonyg@kwominet.or.kr

LATVIA

Center for Research on Women
Institute of Economics
19 Turgeneve Str.
1018 Riga, Latvia
E-mail: spiceina@ac.lza.lv

LEBANON

Institute for Women's Studies in the Arab World
Beirut University College
Box 13–5053
Beirut, Lebanon

Institute for Women's Studies in the Arab World
at the Lebanese American University
Beirut, Lebanon
E-mail: iwsaw@beirut.lau.edu.lb

LESOTHO

Gender and Development Research Program
Institute of Southern African Studies

National University of Lesotho
P.O. Roma 180
Lesotho

LITHUANIA

The Vilnius University Women's Studies Center
Universiteto 3, Room 39
Vilnius 2734, Lithuania
E-mail: msc@cr.vu.lt

MALAYSIA

Asian-Pacific Resources and Research Centre for Women (ARROW)
Persaran
P.O. Box 12224
50770 Kuala Lumpur, Malaysia

Federation of Women Entrepreneurs Association (FEM)
Suite 16.01, Level 16
Menara Tan & Tan, Julan Tun Razak
50400 Kuala Lampur, Malaysia
E-mail: fwem@po.jaring.my
Web site: www.jaring.my/fwem

MEXICO

Centro de Estudios de Genero
Universidad de Guadalajara
Av. Hidalgo 935
Guadalajara, Jalisco, Mexico
E-mail: cande@udgserv.cencar.udg.mx

MONGOLIA

Women's Information and Research Center (WIRC)
Ulaanbaatar, 10th microdistrict
Iapartment 10, room 4
Ulaanbaatar-26, Mongolia
E-mail: wirc@magicnet.mn

NAMIBIA

Interdisciplinary Research Center
University of Namibia
Windhoek, Namibia

NETHERLANDS

Institute for Gender and Multicultural Studies
University of Amsterdam
Rokia 84–90, Amsterdam
E-mail: vanbalen@pscw.uva.nl

NEW CALEDONIA

Pacific Women's Resource Bureau
South Pacific Commission
P.O. Box D5
Noumea Cedex, New Caledonia
E-mail: debbies@spc.org.nc
Web site: www.spc.org.nc

NEW ZEALAND

Department of Women's and Gender Studies
University of Waikoto
Hillcrest Rd. P.B. 3105
Hamilton, New Zealand
E-mail: hlapsley@waikato.ac.nz
Web site: www.waikato.ac.nz/womstud

NIGERIA

National Centre for Women in Development
Better Life Street
Central Area, P.M.B. 185
Garki-Abija, Nigeria

Centre for Gender and Policy
Obafemi Awolowo University
Lfe-lfe
Oyo State, Nigeria

NORWAY

Senter for Kvinneforskning
(Center for Research on Women)
University of Oslo P.B. 1040, Blindern
N 0315 Oslo, Norway
E-mail: s.p.aarseth@sfk.uio.no
Web site: www.uio.no

PAKISTAN

Applied Socio-Economic Research (ASR)
96–1, G Block
Gulberg 111
Lahore, Pakistan
E-mail: iwsl@asr.brain.net.pk

PANAMA

Instituto de Investigación y Capacitación para la Promoción de la Mujer
Apartado Postal 6–5950
El Dorado
Panama, República de Panama

PARAGUAY

Centro Paraguay de Estudio de la Mujer
Facultad de Derechos
Universidad Católica
CC 1718, Asunción, Paraguay

PERU

Flora Tristan Peruvian Women's Center
Parque Hernán Velarde 42
Lima 1, Peru
E-mail: postmaster@flora.org.pe
Web site: www.rcp.net.pe/flora

PHILIPPINES

Center for Women's Resources
#116 Maginhawa Street

Teacher's Village
Quezon City, Philippines

Institute for Women's Studies
P.O. Box 3153
Manila, Philippines

POLAND

Center for the Advancement of Women
00 660 Warszawa
ul Lwowska 17M3, Poland
E-mail: caw-cpk@ikp.atm.com.pl
Web site: www.free.ngo.pl/caw-cpk

ROMANIA

Romanian Society for Feminist Assistance
24 Ferdinand Blvd.
70732, Bucharest, Romania
E-mail: ana@sbnet.ro

RUSSIA

Moscow Center for Gender Studies
32, Nakhimovsky Prospect
Moscow, 117218, Russia
E-mail: mcgs@glasnet.ru

Center for Women in Management
Leningrad Technical University
Polytechnichskaya Str. 29
St. Petersburg, Russia

SENEGAL

Association of African Women for Development
B.P. 3304
Dakar, Senegal

SOUTH AFRICA

Institute for Gender Studies
University of South Africa

P.O. Box 392
Preller Street
Muckleneuk
Pretoria, South Africa 0001
E-mail: lemon@alpha.unisa.ac.29

SPAIN

Centro de Estudios Doña y Sociedad
Mutaner 178 5 Piso #1a
Barcelona, 08036, Spain
E-mail:estudis@redestb.es

SRI LANKA

Pacific Asian Women's Forum
623/27 Rajagiriya Gardens
Colombo, Sri Lanka

SUDAN

Women's Development Center
University of Khartoum
Khartoum, Sudan

SWEDEN

Center for Women and Research on Women
Stockholm University
S-106 91 Stockholm, Sweden
E-mail: aulikki.cederholm@kvinfo.su.se
Web site: www.kvinfo.su.se

TAIWAN

Women's Research Program
Population Studies Center
No. 1, Sec. 4, Roosevelt Road
Taipei, 106, Taiwan R.O.C.
E-mail: psc@ccms.ntu.edu.tw
Web site: www.ms.cc.ntu.edu.tw

TANZANIA

Women's Research and Documentation Project
University of Dar es Salaam
Box 35108
Dar es Salaam, Tanzania

THAILAND

Women's Center and Foundation
P.O. Box 7–47
Bangkok, 10700, Thailand

TRINIDAD AND TOBAGO

Caribbean Association for Feminist Action
P.O. Box 442
Tunapuna, Trinidad and Tobago

TUNISIA

CREDIF
Avenue du Roi Abdelaziz al Saoud, Rue 7131
El Manar II
2092 Tunisie, Tunisia

TURKEY

Implementation Center on the Problems of Women (KASAUM)
University of Ankara
Faculty of Communication
Cebeci, Ankara, Turkey
E-mail: kasaum@media.ankara.edu.tr

UGANDA

Uganda Gender Resource Center
National Theater Complex, 2d Floor
Kampala, Uganda

Faculty of Social Sciences
Makerere University
P.O. Box 7062

Kampala, Uganda
E-mail: gendermu@swiftuganda.com

UKRAINE

Kharkov Gender Studies Center
P.O. Box 244
Kharkov, 310022, Ukraine
E-mail: gender@kgc.kharkov.ua

UNITED KINGDOM

Research Centre on Gender Relations
Leeds Metropolitan University
Leeds
West Yorkshire, LS1 3HE, UK

Change
P.O. Box 823
London, SE24 9JS, UK

Institute of Development Studies
University of Sussex
Falmer
Brighton, BN1 9RE, UK

URUGUAY

Grupo de Estudios sobre la Condición de la Mujer (GRECMU)
Casilla de Correo, 10587
Juan Paullier
1174, Montevideo, Uruguay

UZBEKISTAN

Women's Resource Center
11, Abdulla Kodirig Prosp.
Tashkent, 700 011, Uzbekistan

VIETNAM

Center for Family and Women's Studies
National Center for Social Sciences and Humanities of Vietnam
6 Dinh Cong Trang Street

Hanoi, 844, Vietnam
E-mail: system@cfws.ac.vn

YEMEN

Cultural Development and Project Planning Foundation
Hadda Street
P.O. Box 1892
Republic of Yemen
E-mail: cdppf@y.net.ye

ZIMBABWE

Zimbabwe Women's Resource Center and Network
P.O. Box 2192
Harare, Zimbabwe

NONGOVERNMENTAL ORGANIZATIONS

The following nongovernmental organizations are dedicated the advancement and development of women across the world. Each organization dedicates a substantial amount of its resources to helping promote women entrepreneuers start, sustain, and grow their new businesses.

Arab Women's Forum (AISHA)
East Jerusalem
P.O. Box 54071
East Jerusalem, Israel
E-mail: wscad@netvision.net.il

ASEAN Confederation of Women's Organizations
Malvar Wing, Taft Avenue
P.O. Box 1533
D-708, Metro Manila
Philippines

Association for Women in Development, (AWID)
666 11th Street NW, #540
Washington, DC 200009
E-mail: awid@awid.org

Association of Women Entrepreneurs of Small Scale Industries
37, Velacheri Road
Chennai, 600042, India

Bahai International Community
Office for the Advancement of Women
866 United Nations Plaza Suite 120
New York, N.Y. 10017
E-mail: oaw-ny@bic.org

Disabled People's International
Santiago de Chile
E-mail: pcavada@abello.dic.uchile.cl

Instituto del Tercer Mundo
Jackson 1132
Montevideo 11200
Uruguay

International Federation of Business and Professional Women (IFBPW)
Studio 16, Cloisters Business Center, 8 Battersea Park Road
London, SW8 4BG, UK
E-mail: bqwithq@compuserve.com

Latin American Committee for the Defense of Women's Rights
Avenida Estados Unidos 1295, Dpto 702
Lima, 11, Peru

Pan-African Women's Organization
B.P. 765
Rua dos Conquieros 37/39
Luanda, Angola

Women's Intercultural Network
1950 Hayes Street #2
San Fransisco, CA 94417
E-mail: win@win-cawa.org
Website: www.win-cawa.org

Women's International Democratic Federation
25, Rue du Charolais
Paris, 75012, France
E-mail: fdif@fdif.eu.org
Website: www.fdif.eu.org

Women's Union of Russia
Glinishevsky by-str. 6
Moscow, 103832, Russia

Women's World Banking
8 West 40th Street, 10th Floor
New York, NY 10018

Working Women's Forum (India)
55 Bhimasena Garden Road, Mylapore
Chennal, Tamilnadu, 600004, India

World Association of Women Entrepreneurs
Immeuble Yasmine, Apt. 1–1
Les Berges du Lac
Tunis, 1180, Tunisia
E-mail: wpresd.fcem@planet.tn
Web site: www.fcem.org

World Union of Catholic Women's Organizations
18, Rue Notre Dame des Champs
Paris, 75006, France
E-mail: wucwoparis@wanadoo.fr
Website: www.wucwo.org

Worldwide Network—Women in Development
6005, 32d Street, NW
Washington, DC 20015
E-mail: jclones@tmn.com

Worldwide Organization for Women (WOW)
210 East 21st Street, #3B
New York, NY 10010

World Young Women's Christian Association (World YWCA)
16, Ancienne Route, Grand Saconnex
Geneva, 1218, Switzerland
E-mail: worldoffice@worldywca.org
Website: www.worldywca.org

UNITED NATIONS SITES

The following Web sites provide information on United Nations programs designed to empower women and encourage female entrepreneurship.

United Nations Development Program (UNDP): www.undp.org

Gender in Development Program at UNDP: www.undp.org/gender

Women Watch, the UN Gateway for the Advancement and Empowerment of Women: www.un.org/womenwatch

United Nations Division for the Advancement of Women (DAW): www.
un.org/womenwatch/daw

The United Nations Development Fund for Women: www.unfem.undp.org

The United Nations Research and Training Institute for the Advancement
of Women: www.un-instraw.org

MULTILATERAL AND REGIONAL
DEVELOPMENT BANKS AND ORGANIZATIONS

Loosely associated with the United Nations are the World Bank
and the International Monetary Fund, two large, powerful organizations whose purpose is to assist in development in the less modern
areas of the world. In addition, there are four regional development
organizations with similar objectives.

In addition to being possible financing sources, directly or indirectly, the international development banks through their many projects also offer numerous supply opportunities for female
entrepreneurs. The banks produce publications indicating their procurement needs.

The World Bank
1818 H Street NW
Washington, DC 20433
USA

The primary goal of the World Bank and its affiliates is to raise the
standard of living in developing countries. The bank finances a broad
range of capital infrastructure projects, but it particularly focuses on
investments that improve the quality of life of the masses. It also
promotes economic development and structural reform in the countries in which it is involved. There are two parts of the bank, the
International Bank for Reconstruction and Development (IBRD) and
the International Development Association (IDA), both of which lend
funds, give advice, and try to get investments moving. The IDA specifically concentrates on the poorer countries and provides easier financial terms. An affiliate, the International Finance Corporation,
works directly with the private sector. It invests its own funds as well
as seeks out other monies for commercial enterprises. Another affiliate is the Multilateral Investment Guarantee Agency, which seeks to
protect the investor from political risks.

The World Bank will speak with you and may produce or lead you to your needed financing. The bank has offices throughout the world, but Washington, D.C., is the location of its world headquarters. The bank also publishes the *International Business Opportunities Service*, to which you can subscribe by contacting World Bank Publications at Room T8094 at the above address.

International Finance Corporation (IFC)
1818 H Street NW
Room I 9163
Washington, DC 20433
USA

The IFC is an institution within the World Bank group that provides support to the private sector in its effort to promote growth in developing countries. It invests in commercial enterprises. If interested, companies should contact the corporate relations unit to make proposals or obtain information.

Multilateral Investment Guarantee Agency (MIGA)
1818 H Street NW
Washington, DC 20433
USA

The MIGA provides guarantees against loss from noncommercial risks in foreign investment.

International Monetary Fund (IMF)
700 19th Street NW
Washington, DC 20431
USA

If you want detailed information about the financial stability and performance of countries and their economies, you may want to explore the many publications of the International Monetary Fund. In particular, the monthly magazine, accompanied by an annual yearbook, *Information Financial Statistics*, contains a wealth of economic data difficult to come by elsewhere.

Inter-American Development Bank
1300 New York Avenue NW
Washington, DC 20577
USA

The Inter-American Development Bank (IDB) was established in 1959 and focuses on the economic and social development in Latin America and the Caribbean. The IDB supplements private funds as needed to support development in the borrowing member countries. Like the World Bank and IMF, it may provide technical advice to the government of the countries in which it is working. Projects are quite varied and include sewage treatment, road construction, support for entrepreneurs, education and training, farming, and fishing.

African Development Bank Headquarters
01 BP 1387
Abidjan 01
Côte d'Ivoire

The African Development Bank seeks to aid the development of African member nations by financing projects and promoting private investment in Africa. Related to the bank is the African Development Fund, which provides financing to the poorer countries of Africa at especially low rates.

Asian Development Bank
P.O. Box 780
1099 Manila, Philippines
street address:
6 ADB Avenue, Mandaluyong
Metro Manila, Philippines

With the past progress in several Asian countries, the Asian Development Bank is planning to focus its resources on specific needy nations in the area. The bank mostly finances and supports infrastructure projects.

European Bank for Reconstruction and Development
One Exchanges Square
London EC2A 2EH UK

The European Bank for Reconstruction and Development was established in 1991 to aid in the development and transition of the countries of Central and Eastern Europe and the former Soviet Union. The bank seeks to promote private initiative. It can make loans to private enterprise, invest in equity capital, and confirm guarantees.

European Investment Bank
100 Bd Konrad Adenauer
L-2950 Luxembourg
Grand Duchy of Luxembourg

The mission of the European Investment Bank is to further the objectives of the European Union by making long-term financing available for sound investments. Financing is often provided in the form of individual loans and global loans to assist with development in Africa, Latin America and the Caribbean, Eastern and Central Europe, Asia, and the Mediterranean.

The European Development Fund
European Commission
Directorate General for Development
General Financial Affairs; Relations with European Investment Bank
Rue de la Loi, 200
B-1040 Brussels, Belgium

The European Development Fund is the main financing instrument of the Lome Convention and provides grants to aid programs for the seventy African, Caribbean, and Pacific countries that are signatories to this agreement with the European Union.

Phare Programme
European Commission, Information Unit
Directorate General External Relations
Europe and the New Independent States MO 34 3/80
Westraat 200 Rue de la Loi
B-1049 Brussels, Belgium
E-mail: phare.info@dgla.cec.be
Web site: www.cec.lu/en/comm/dgla/phare.html

The Phare Programme is a European Union initiative that supports the development of a larger democratic family of nations within a prosperous and stable Europe. Phare provides know-how from a wide range of noncommercial public and private organizations to its partner countries. It acts as a multiplier by stimulating investment and responding to needs that cannot be met by others. Phare can facilitate the release of funds for important projects from other donors through studies, capital grants, guarantee schemes, and credit lines.

TACIS
European Commission
Tacis Information Office
Directorate General for External Political Relations
AN 88 1/06
Westraat 200 Rue de la Loi
B-1049 Brussels, Belgium

The Tacis Programme is a European Union initiative to help the Newly Independent States move away from centrally planned to market economies. It provides support in the form of grants to foster exchange of knowledge and expertise through partnerships, links, and networks.

EUROPEAN OFFICES OF COMMERCE

This list of European government Web sites and offices provides a starting point for those wishing to locate and explore citizen-oriented information on female entrepreneurship disseminated by the European governments.

Austria: http://gov.austria-info.

Belgium: http://www.online.be/belgium

Denmark: http://www.SDN.DK

Finland: http://www.vn.fi

France: http://www.france.diplomatie.fr

Germany: http://www.auswaertiges-amt.government.de

Germany (Bavaria): http://www.bayern.de

Greece: http://web.ariadne-t.gr

Ireland: http://www.ir/gov.ie

Italy: http://www.aipa.it

Luxembourg: http://www.restena.lv

Netherlands: http://145.10.251.249

Portugal: http://infocid.sma.pt

Spain: http://www.la-moncloa.es

Sweden: http://www.sb.gov.se

United Kingdom: http://www.open.gov.UK

Ministry of Economics
Stubenrint 1
1010 Vienna
Austria

Department of Commerce
Yves Galland
139 Rue de Bercy
75572 Paris, Cdex 12
France

Ministry of Economic Affairs
Villemombler Stra 76
53123 Bonn
Germany

Ministry of Commerce
Kanigos Square
Athens
Greece

Ministry of Commerce
Arnarhavali
150 Reykjavik
Iceland

Department of Commerce
Kildare Street
Dublin 2
Ireland
Web site: www.irlgov.ie/dtt

Ministero del Commercio
Viale America 341
001 44 Rome
Italy

Minister of the Economy
19 Boulevard Royale
2914 Luxembourg
Grand Duchy of Luxembourg

Ministry of Trade and Commerce
P.O. Box 8148 DEP
0033 Oslo
Norway

Ministry of Trade and Commerce
1033 Stockholm
Sweden

Department of Trade and Industry
Ashdown House
123 Victoria Street
London SW1E 6RB
United Kingdom

UNITED STATES RESOURCES FOR WOMEN ENTREPRENEURS (BY STATE)

The leading national organization for women buisness owners in the United States is NAWBO (National Association of Women Business Owners). Although they have offices in almost every state, they are best contacted through their national headquarters at

1595 Spring Hill Road, Suite 330
Vienna, VA 22182
E-mail: national@nawbo.org
Web site: www.nawbo.org

The Center for Women's Business Research, founded as the National Foundation for Women Business Owners, provides research to document the economic and social contributions of woman-owned firms and also provides consulting and public-relations services.

Center for Women's Business Research
1411 K Street, NW, Suite 1350
Washington, DC 20005–3407 USA
E-mail: info@womensbusinessresearch.org
Web site: www.womensbusinessresearch.org

ALABAMA

Women's Business Assistance Center, Inc. (WBAC)
1301 Azalea Road, Suite 201A
Mobile, AL 36693
E-mail: wbac@ceebic.org
Web site: ceebic.org/wbac

The Women's Business Assistance Center—a private nonprofit corporation—is in the Center for Entrepreneurial Excellence, a former school campus, which was purchased and renovated by the City of Mobile and Mobile County. It is now a business incubator and training center. The executive director of the WBAC is also owner of the

Women's Yellow Pages of the Gulf Coast. The WBAC provides training seminars and one-on-one counseling for south Alabama and northwest Florida.

ALASKA

The YWCA of Anchorage
WOMEN$ Fund
245 West Fifth Avenue
Anchorage, AK 99510–2059
E-mail: ywcaak@Alaska.NET

WOMEN$ Fund was established in 1995 as a program of the YWCA and fully implemented in the spring of 1996. WOMEN$ Fund is a microenterprise training and microlending program for women entrepreneurs in Anchorage, Alaska. Consistent with the national YWCA's mission to empower women and girls and to eliminate racism, the programs of the YWCA of Anchorage promote independence, knowledge, and self-esteem, especially for low-income and minority women. WOMEN$ Fund's mission is to secure financial independence for women by providing capital and technical assistance. The organization's individual mentoring, training classes in entrepreneurship, technical assistance, and seed money for women-owned small businesses, empowers low- and moderate-income single-parent and minority women in Anchorage and surrounding Alaska communities through economic self-sufficiency.

ARIZONA

Southern Arizona Women's Fund
3610 North Prince Village Place, Suite 100
Tucson, AZ 85719–2099

Self-Employment Loan Fund, Inc. (SELF)
201 N. Central Avenue, Suite CC10
Phoenix, AZ 85073–1000
E-mail: SELF@uswest.net

SELF provides training, technical assistance, and access to loans for low-income individuals, primarily women and minorities, who are starting or expanding small businesses. The training sessions last ten or fourteen weeks, with the outcome of a completed business plan.

Upon successful completion of the training component, participants are eligible to join a "Borrowers Circle" in order to access funds through SELF's peer lending process. Borrowers Circles of three to eight individuals provide an avenue for support, loan repayment, and continuing business education. Individuals who have been in business for two years or more and have an acceptable business plan may be eligible for larger loans through SELF's Individual Lending Program. SELF currently serves all Maricopa County and the Gila River Indian Community. The population of Maricopa County is urban and is home to more than half the state's population. The Gila River Indian Community occupies 372,000 acres in south-central Arizona, south of Phoenix, and has high unemployment and few opportunities for nascent entrepreneurs. SELF participants are 66 percent women, 72 percent low-income, and ethnically diverse: 65 percent are minorities—20 percent Hispanic, 41 percent African American, 3 percent Native American, and 1 percent Asian American.

ARKANSAS

Arkansas Enterprise Group
2304 W 29th Avenue
Pine Bluff, AR 71603
Telephone: 870–535–6233
E-mail: ARWBDC@ehbt.com

The Arkansas Women's Business Development Center (ARWBDC) is located in Pine Bluff, "the Gateway to the Delta." The program was funded in September 1999 to provide education, training, and technical assistance to woman-owned businesses, focusing mainly on minorities. From 1988 to 1998, more than 30 percent of the participants in the entrepreneurship programs were on some form of public assistance. Programs include FastTrac entrepreneurial training, currently being held in Forrest City and Pine Bluff, Arkansas. A women's business mentoring program provides advanced business training for women who have been in business for at least one year. The program also helps in developing relationships with mentors who provide advice on general business matters. Because of the high demand for child care there is also a special module for childcare providers. Other services include assistance with loan packaging and special workshops, which including Internet training and money-management seminars.

CALIFORNIA

Los Angeles Women's Foundation
6030 Wilshire Boulevard, Suite 303
Los Angeles, CA 90036
Web site: www.lawf.org

Shaler Adams Foundation
P.O. Box 29274
San Francisco, CA 94129–0274

Renaissance Entrepreneurship Center
275 Fifth Street
San Francisco, CA 94103–4120
E-mail: janet@rencenter.org

Renaissance comprises a unique multicultural marketplace of entrepreneurs. Diversity—ethnic, social, and economic—is a critical factor for the center's success. The diversity generates a synergy that translates to business income: 60 percent of Renaissance graduates report doing business with one another. A ten-year impact study by the Federal Reserve Board of San Francisco in 1997 revealed that 87 percent of businesses started through this program are still in operation (compared to the national average of 38 percent). Services include an incubator facility, loan packaging and links to credit resources, core business planning, introduction to business, and advanced action-planning classes. Graduates of Renaissance programs receive a one-year free membership in the San Francisco Chamber of Commerce, peer support, mentoring, events, and a business expo.

Women's Enterprise Development Corporation (WEDC)
235 East Broadway, Suite 506
Long Beach, CA 90802
E-mail: wedc@aol.com

WEDC, previously known as California AWED, began in 1989 with Small Business Administration funding to assist the growing number of women business owners in Los Angeles. It has been awarded a new grant to meet the needs of the San Gabriel Valley area of southern California. The center will focus on serving the fast-growing Latina and Asian populations, with training offered in Spanish, Mandarin, Cantonese, Khmer, Vietnamese, Armenian, and English. Programs and activities include entrepreneurial training at the start-up, midsize, and rapid-growth levels; meetings and consultations; procurement and contracting assistance; direct microlending assistance and assistance in procuring SBA loans; and entrepreneurship services for youths. In addition to a full-time facility, WEDC uses a "circuit rider" project manager for outreach, to provide counseling within communities. WEDC also employs a "biz-tic" for business counseling that lays out a program for each student and then enables her to understand the end goal of the engagement, the steps necessary to get to that goal, and the benefits of each step.

Women's Initiative for Self-Employment (WI)
450 Mission Street, Suite 402
San Francisco, CA 94105
E-mail: womensinitsf@igc.apc.org

Spanish Site
1398 Valencia St.
San Francisco, CA 94110
E-mail: wialas@igc.apc.org

Oakland
11611 Telegraph Ave., Suite 702
Oakland, CA 94612
E-mail: wioakland@igc.apc.org

The Women's Initiative (WI) began in 1987 as a means to provide low-income women with the tools and resources to begin and expand businesses. The programs are provided in both English and Spanish. WI provides a comprehensive package of business training, personal development workshops, credit counseling, start-up and expansion financing, business counseling, peer group support, and mentoring.

West Company
367 North State Street, Suite 201
Ukiah, CA 95482
E-mail: westco@pacific.net

Fort Bragg
306 East Redwood Avenue, Suite 2
Fort Bragg, CA 95437
E-mail: westcofb@mcn.org

West Company serves microenterprise owners in rural northern California, targeting low-income women and minorities. West Company provides business planning and management assistance at any stage of business ownership from feasibility through expansion. Services include business plan training, individual consulting, access to capital through individual and peer loans, business network formation, and assistance with business applications using technology.

COLORADO

Mi Casa Career Development and Business Center for Women
Denver, CO 80204
E-mail: acarroll@micasadenver.org
Web site: www.micasadenver.org

Founded in 1976, Mi Casa Resource Center for Women provides quality employment and education services that promote economic independence for low-income, predominantly Latina women and youth. Services include educational counseling, job-readiness and job-search training, life-skills development, job placement, and non-traditional and computer skills training. Entrepreneurial training is provided through either the Evening Entrepreneurial Training Program or Project Success. Individuals learn how to start a business and develop a business plan, with microloans available to program graduates. Youth development, dropout prevention, leadership training, and responsible decision making are provided through three youth programs: Mi Carrera (My Career), Mi Camina (My Road), and Fenix (teen pregnancy, AIDS, and STD prevention program). Mi Casa has received a new grant to expand their services to Colorado Springs with a satellite program in Pueblo, a predominantly Hispanic community. There are few employment opportunities in Pueblo except low-wage hourly service and retail positions, and many women have a difficult time achieving and sustaining self-sufficiency. Mi Casa collaborates with the Women's Resource Agency to provide services. Mi Casa offers training geared specifically toward women on public assistance and also offers their evening program in Spanish. Monthly seminars are open to clients and graduates of their training programs and mentoring is available through Tuesday Tune-Up seminars and weekend roundtables. Mi Casa provides transportation and child-care assistance as well as clothing and other emergency services.

CONNECTICUT

Connecticut Permanent Commission of Women
18–20 Trinity Street
Hartford, CT 06106
E-mail: pcsw@po.state.ct.us
Web site: www.cga.state.ct.us/pcsw

The Entrepreneurial Center of Hartford's College for Women at the University of Hartford
50 Elizabeth Street
Hartford, CT 06105
E-mail: sbaowboct@mail.hartford.edu

The Entrepreneurial Center serves potential start-up and established women business owners throughout Connecticut, with special emphasis on women who are socially and economically disadvantaged. The center is a collaboration between People's Bank and the Connecticut Development Authority. The University of Hartford provides the self-assessment workshops and conducts a 16-week intensive business training program. People's Bank and the Connecticut Development Authority provide assistance in seeking access to capital. The center offers the "Trickle-Up Program," an international fund that provides seed capital up to $750 to qualified clients for startup, a grant that does not have to be paid back. The center provides technical assistance for all graduates for the life cycles of their businesses, collaborating statewide with economic development organizations. This program is the first in the United States to link a state agency, a private corporation, and a university in a formal partnership.

Women's Business Development Center (WBDC)
400 Main Street, Suite 500
Stamford, CT 06901
E-mail: wbdc@ferg.lib.ct.us

WBDC serves women from all social and economic backgrounds in southwest Connecticut and collaborates with other community agencies to target socially and economically disadvantaged clients. In addition to one-on-one counseling, the training courses include "Finance a Business," "Launch a Business," and "The Business Toolbox," as well as "The Experienced Entrepreneur: Leveraging Growth,

Government Procurement" and "Camp Entrepreneur: A Mother/ Daughter Experience." Collaborating with the Urban League of Southwestern Connecticut, Inc., and the YWCA of Greenwich, WBDC is developing an innovative summer camp program for girls between the ages of 11 and 14.

DELAWARE

MicroBusiness Chamber of Commerce (MBCC)
Olakunle S. Oludina, Director
233 King Street
Wilmington, DE 19801
E-mail: info@microbusinesschamber.com
Web site: www.microbusinesschamber.com

The MBCC, a full-service chamber tailor-made for small businesses owned by women and minorities, is a joint partnership of the YWCA of New Castle County, the SBA's Office of Women's Business Ownership, and the Delaware State Chamber of Commerce. MBCC offers professional development seminars, including marketing, business/financial management, and sales development. It also offers individual Internet training and counseling. Its various events, offer opportunities to network with other business owners, big and small. Examples of its promotional activites are a free business profile on the Internet and an online resource center, which provides information to support small businesses and links to other sites that may be useful to the small business owner. In cooperation with the other programs of the YWCA, participants have access to microloans, homeownership, and savings assistance.

DISTRICT OF COLUMBIA

American Psychological Association—Women's Program Office
750 First Street, NE
Washington, DC 20002
E-mail: gkeita@apa.org
Web site: www.apa.org/pi/wpo

American Sociological Association—Committee of the Status of Women
1722 N Street NW
Washington, DC 20036

Women's Business Center, Inc.
1001 Connecticut Avenue NW, Suite 312
Washington, DC 20036
E-mail: beth@womensbusinesscenter.org
Web site: www.womensbusinesscenter.org

The national Women's Business Center has two locations, one in
downtown D.C. and a second that shares office space with the SBA's
Washington, D.C., district office and the small business development
subcenter to maximize access to their business services. The center
offers "Introduction to Business Ownership," "Up and Running,"
"Managing a Business with Accountability," "Doing Business with the
Government," "The Business Council," "The Roundtable," "The
Business Laboratory," and "The Bottom Line." There is also an Online WBC, which was developed on behalf of the U.S. Small Business
Administration's Office of Women's Business Ownership (OWBO)
and several corporate sponsors, who joined forces in a public/private
partnership. This "virtual women's business center" is an extension
of the SBA women's business centers throughout the United States.
It works in unison with them to provide timely and topical information, training, individual counseling, and opportunities for online
networking to women business owners anywhere, any time. The combined efforts of the WBCs and OWBO create unlimited possibilities
for reaching women who want access to information, personal guidance, and insight into business-management skills, particularly those
who do not have a WBC nearby or who cannot visit one during
operating hours. In less than a year and a half, the Online WBC
reached users in more than 100 countries and had received more than
2 million hits; it currently receives about a million hits per month.

FLORIDA

Women's Business Center (WBC) of Northwest Florida
6235 N. Davis Highway, Suite 111B
Pensacola, FL 32504
E-mail: womenbiz@bellsouth.net

The Women's Business Center of Northwest Florida serves practicing and potential women business owners, with an emphasis on socially and economically disadvantaged women. The WBC serves the
most populous counties in the Panhandle: Escambia, Santa Rosa, and

Okaloosa. Military bases, such as Eglin Air Force Base and Pensacola Naval Air Station, bring many military spouses and retirees to the area. The WBC targets these two groups, especially women retiring from the military who are considering business ownership as a second career. The WBC offers training, counseling, mentoring, and video-conferencing in the Fort Walton Beach area. The WBC, established in August of 1999, is a project of the Women's Business Assistance Center, Inc., of Mobile, Alabama.

GEORGIA

Greater Atlanta Small Business Project (GRASP)
55 Marietta Street, Suite 2000
Atlanta, GA 30303
E-mail: m_coakley@graspnet.org

GRASP gives a hand up to women in Atlanta and Fulton County, about half of whom are African American. GRASP offers three program tracks, designed for the needs and preferences of each woman: "The New Horizon Track" is a hands-on business-development program for women making a transition from welfare to work. "The Education/Training/Information Track" offers Internet and other computer training and access, a small business resource center, access to training programs of numerous other small business service providers, and twice-monthly workshops on topics of interest to women and not otherwise available. "The Advanced Business Performance Track" invests intensive management and technical assistance to well-established women-owned businesses that have growth potential, which can include startups with unusually strong management capacity or a unique market niche. The team assigned to each client comprises an experienced, successful businessperson, an accountant, and an attorney. GRASP partners with TEKnowledge, Inc., a minority-owned technology firm that responds to user questions and problems on technology or other issues. In addition, GRASP operates a cooperative that markets products and services of women-owned businesses to corporations, government procurement offices, and certain consumer markets.

Women's Economic Development Agency (WEDA)
675 Ponce de Leon Avenue
Atlanta, GA 30308

The WEDA program offers a five-hour seminar series for women business owners and provides mentoring and one-on-one counseling. Most clients are African American women, but the program is open to all individuals. Topics covered in the training program are marketing, business planning, accounting and finance, contract negotiation, and domestic and international procurement.

HAWAII

Hawaii Women's Business Center
1111 Bishop Street, #204
Honolulu, HI 96813

The economic crisis in Asia has hit Hawaii's tourism market hard; its impact pervades numerous other industries. With experience in working with Samoan, Fijian, Hawaiian, Korean, Japanese, Filipino, and Chinese populations, the Hawaii Women's Business Center is well positioned to serve the ethnically and culturally diverse Hawaiian population. The business center's program gives each client an individual assessment followed by training in writing business plans, a marketing study group, and a monthly networking and information meeting. The center offers workshops on special topics such as "Designing Brochures and Flyers," "Taxes for the Small Business Owner," "Taking the 'Starving' Out of Artist," and "Starting a Home-Based Business." The center has also entered into a partnership with the Chamber of Commerce of Hawaii to provide distance and correspondence training. Within five years WFRC plans to have subcenters on at least two other islands.

IDAHO

Women's Entrepreneurial Mentoring Systems, Inc. (WEMS)
P.O. Box 6700
Boise, ID 83707–0700
E-mail: frontdesk@wemswbc.org

WEMS serves all women in the state, with special outreach to socially and economically disadvantaged clients. Specific outreach plans are proposed for finding, assisting, and encouraging women who own or wish to start home-based businesses. Programs to support women with disabilities who want to start businesses are also offered. Some training is provided by WEMS, while other assistance is provided through the Business Initiative Corporation (BIC), OSCS, the Service Corps of Retired Executives (SCORE), the Small Business Development Center (SBDC), and the Boise Chamber of Commerce, all of which share the facility. WEMS is a product of the Women's Network for Entrepreneurial Training (WNET) Program and provides a monthly Mini-WNET mentoring group online.

ILLINOIS

Chicago Commission on Women
500 North Pestigo, Room 6B
Chicago, IL 60611

Women's Business Development Center (WBDC)
8 South Michigan Avenue, Suite 400
Chicago, IL 60603
E-mail: wbdc@aol.com

Founded in 1986, WBDC serves women business owners in the greater Chicago area and advocates for women business owners nationwide. Since 1989 the WBDC has helped establish women's business centers in Illinois, Ohio, Florida, Pennsylvania, and Massachusetts. WBDC provides entrepreneurial training courses and seminars, one-on-one counseling, financial assistance and loan packaging for microloans, SBA and other government loan programs, mentoring, Women-owned Business Enterprises (WBE) certification, and procurement assistance. The center hosts an annual conference and buyers' mart. Part of its advocacy program is policy development for women's economic and business issues. Strategic alliances with private and public partners extend WBDC's reach to the neediest communities. WBDC provides services through a local bank's "Wheels of Business" van, which travels to low-income neighborhoods to offer training and counseling.

INDIANA

Fort Wayne's Women's Bureau, Inc. (FWWBI)
3521 Lake Avenue, Suite 1
Fort Wayne, IN 46805
E-mail: info@womensenterprise.org
Web site: www.womensenterprise.org

FWWBI serves Fort Wayne and nine counties in northeastern Indiana, six of which are part of the Fort Wayne metropolitan area and three that are primarily rural. They reach out to low-income and Hispanic women and women with disabilities. FWWBI offers comprehensive training on finance, management, marketing, and government procurement and runs a two-part course, "Owning Your Business." They provide workshops and training, including all the services of the SBA, through the SBA home page and the online Women's Business Center (WBC). They offer full-time bilingual services for all program areas. FWWBI works with AARP to identify ways the program can meet the unique needs of senior women who need or want to continue working and want to explore entrepreneurship. In cooperation with local services, they provide signing interpreters for the hearing impaired and transportation for people with physical disabilities.

IOWA

Institute for Social and Economic Development (ISED)
1901 Broadway, Suite 313
Iowa City, IA 52240
E-mail: cpigsley@ised.org
Web site: www.ised.org

ISED is a consortium of all the major business-development organizations in the state; it serves every level of women business owners from start-up to high growth. The consortium maintains offices in six cities and fifteen Small Business Development Center (SBDC) subcenters. The nonprofit ISED has a long history of providing self-employment training programs, especially to the socially and economically disadvantaged.

KENTUCKY

Midway College
512 East Stephens Street
Midway, KY 40347–1120
E-mail: jmarkham@midway.edu

The current service area includes the Lexington metropolitan area and the rural Danville–Boyle County area; from these the program plans to expand to other areas of the state by distance learning and other techniques. The college works in close coordination with local agencies to reach out to welfare-to-work, low-income, and minority populations. Midway coordinates with other women's colleges that have SBA-funded women's business centers—Columbia College in South Carolina and the University of the Sacred Heart in Puerto Rico. Programs include "Taking Off: Launching Your Small Business," "Advancing Your Business," technical workshops on selling to the government, sources of capital, mentoring, and team building. In addition to offering a directory of online computer training programs, they provide discussion groups for small office/home office businesses. Minutes of quarterly mentoring meetings and transcripts of events are posted online where participants can continue discussions or those unable to attend can join in. They also provide specific interactive course materials and an online business library page with recommended readings and resources and links to discounted materials. Midway College will present an annual award for outstanding achievement by a woman entrepreneur in Kentucky that will include an invitation to an honorary fellowship to speak at college events during the next year.

LOUISIANA

Women Entrepreneurs for Economic Development, Inc. (WEED)
1683 North Claiborne Avenue, Suite 101
New Orleans, LA 70116
E-mail: webc@bellsouth.net

Located in a historic district that includes one of the largest strips of abandoned commercial properties in New Orleans, the center has assisted women in Orleans Parish since 1988. It provides business training and counseling, one-on-one Internet and computer training, basic life-skills training, housing and family services, and a business incubator. Its "NxLevel for Business Start-ups" offers a hands-on, commonsense approach to developing a small business. WEED also operates a child-care facility, a Family Day Care Home Program, and a thrift shop that provides low-cost working wardrobes to clients. WEED collaborates with the Housing Authority of New Orleans to make low-interest loans available to NxLevel graduates who live in public housing and to make microloans available to residents with small businesses.

MAINE

Women's Business Development Program (WBDP)
P.O. Box 268
Wiscasset, ME 04578
E-mail: efg@ceimaine.org
Web site: www.ceimaine.org

Coastal Enterprises, Inc. (CEI), is a private nonprofit community development corporation that provides financing and technical assistance to Maine businesses that in turn provide income, ownership, or employment opportunities to low-income people. WBDP emerged from CEI's experience in assessing women business owners' needs, and providing women business owners with training, technical assistance, financing, and advocacy. Statewide in scope, the project targets assistance to women who have started their businesses. Project participants benefit from CEI's capacity to provide access to capital through its SBA MicroLoan Program and Loan Prequalification programs and its other resources.

MARYLAND

The Mid-Atlantic Equity Center
5454 Wisconsin Avenue
Suite 655
Chevy Chase, Maryland 20815
E-mail: equity@maex.org
Web site: www.maec.org

Women's Business Institute, Inc. (WBI)
10 S. Howard Street, 6th Floor
Baltimore, MD 21201
E-mail: checket@juno.com

WBI will serve start-up and established businesses, including those owned by socially and economically disadvantaged women in rural communities in Maryland, West Virginia, and Pennsylvania. Services include one-on-one counseling, Internet training, "First Step" for welfare-to-work clients, the two-part "Premier FastTrac," "Contracting Dollar$ and Sense," and "Entrepreneurship 101," as well as loan packaging and mentoring. Each participant receives a training manual and a booklet that contains printouts from the Online Women's Business Center and lists of Internet addresses with brief content descriptions pertinent to the program. The center will investigate how to modernize its distance learning programs by partnering with universities, colleges, and learning centers.

Women Entrepreneurs of Baltimore, Inc. (WEB)
1118 Light Street, Suite 202
Baltimore, MD 21230
E-mail: aczinn@connext.net

WEB, a non-profit organization, is an entrepreneurial training program designed to help economically disadvantaged women become self-sufficient through business development. The main components of the WEB program are an intensive three-month business-skills course, mentoring, financing strategy development, community networking, resource sharing, and professional business consultation.

MASSACHUSETTS

Center for Women and Work
883 Broadway Street, Room 212A
Lowell, MA 01854
E-mail: jean_pyle@uml.edu

Center for Women and Enterprise, Inc.
1135 Tremont Street, Suite 480
Boston, MA 02108
E-mail: info@cweboston.org

The Center for Women and Enterprise, Inc., is a nonprofit educational organization whose mission is to empower women to become economically self-sufficient and prosperous through entrepreneurship. The first center of its kind in Massachusetts, CWE provides courses, workshops, roundtables, one-on-one consulting, and loan packaging assistance to women who seek to start or grow their own businesses.

MICHIGAN

Women's Life Insurance Society
1338 Military

Port Huron. MI 48061–5020
E-mail: wkrabach@womenslifeins.com
Web site: www.womenslifeins.com

Detroit Entrepreneurship Institute, Inc. (DEI)
455 W. Fort Street, 4th Floor
Detroit, MI 48226
E-mail: deibus@aol.com

DEI serves businesses owned by welfare recipients, dislocated workers, and other women with low to moderate incomes who are seeking
self-sufficiency through entrepreneurship. Two of DEI's long-term
(eleven-week) classes are "Self-Employment Initiative," open to welfare recipients, and "Enterprise Development Initiative," open to the
low- and moderate-income general public, dislocated workers, and
women with disabilities. The State of Michigan partnered with
CFED, the Corporation for Enterprise Development, an organization that supports programs for low-income and distressed communities, and secured a two-year waiver to protect the welfare benefits
of DEI participants. The waiver allows participants to earn business
income and accumulate assets while continuing to receive their grants
and medical benefits during the start-up phase of their businesses.

Center for Empowerment and Economic Development (CEED)
2002 Hogback Road, Suite 12
Ann Arbor, MI 48105
E-mail: mrichards@wwnet.net

Grand Rapids Opportunities for Women (GROW)
25 Sheldon SE, Suite 210
Grand Rapids, MI 49503
E-mail: rvanderven@growbusiness.org

Grand Rapids Opportunities for Women (GROW) is a nonprofit
economic development organization that provides women from diverse backgrounds with opportunities to develop the skills and acquire
the knowledge needed to achieve financial independence. Focusing
on small businesses, GROW provides entrepreneurial training and
the follow-up services needed to sustain and expand a business. Since
starting a business often affects all aspects of a woman's life, GROW
is committed to providing group and individual support for both business and personal development. GROW's economic-development
programming has three components: business readiness assessment,

entrepreneurial training/business plan development, and follow-up services. GROW offers a fifteen-week course, "Minding Your Own Business," which covers accounting, bookkeeping, taxes, marketing, financial analysis, sales techniques, promotion, inventory, conflict management, trade shows, business writing, public speaking, and market research. Follow-up services include business circles, "Up-Close" seminars, a marketing fund, technical assistance, networking opportunities, and the Mercantile Bank/GROW Step Loan and Savings Program.

A new offering at GROW is the Economic Literacy Program, a four-session course about money management and saving. Economic Literacy is the prerequisite for opening a GROW Individual Development Account (IDA), a matched savings account dedicated to helping women build assets—as opposed to debt—in order to start or expand a business, purchase housing, or finance education.

MINNESOTA

Minnesota Women's Business Center (MWBC)
226 East 1st Street
Fosston, MN 56542
E-mail: wind@means.net

The MWBC provides technical assistance to new and existing businesses. Services are provided through one-on-one counseling, classroom training (using a variety of workshop formats), and an annual regional women's business conference. It networks with several organizations to extend its reach. MWBC also provides training services to twelve rural counties in northwestern Minnesota in collaboration with the Northwest Minnesota Foundation.

MISSISSIPPI

Mid-Delta Women's Entrepreneurial Training and
Technical Assistance Program (WE-TAP)
119 South Theobald Street
Greenville, MS 38701

Mississippi Action for Community Education (MACE) oversees WE-TAP. Given the limited opportunities for traditional employment in the Delta, WE-TAP creates nontraditional means of economic support for low-income women. For more than thirty years MACE has been in the forefront of economic development initiatives in the Delta. WE-TAP expanded upon the New Enterprise for Women (Project New, a business incubator project) and supports small business development using their women's entrepreneurial program, Project Jump Start. MACE has a long history working with the undereducated poor, most of whom are women who will lose public assistance under welfare reform. They have very poor prospects for gainful employment through traditional means. The ultimate goal is to create self-sufficiency and build wealth, particularly among low-income women in the Mississippi Delta.

MISSOURI

Grace Hill Neighborhood Services
2600 Hadley
St. Louis, MO 63106

Grace Hill's service areas consist entirely of impoverished neighborhoods with residents at or below poverty level, high crime and high school dropout rates, evident drug and gang presence, and deteriorating properties. The project's serves St. Louis and three counties. The project's first concern is outreach and marketing to make women aware of their services. Long-term training for start-up and existing businesses is subcontracted through a small business development center. Grace Hill runs a business incubator and provides a list of approved local suppliers who offer discounts to women business owners. The project is also compiling a list of women's businesses so that the woman can patronize one another's companies (Grace Hill hopes to expand the list into a nationwide database). Because of their special focus on welfare-to-work participants and low-income working women, the project will hold a monthly online chat group of disadvantaged clients from around the country.

MONTANA

Career Training Institute
347 North Last Chance Gulch
Helena, MT 59601
E-mail: mgarrity@ixi.net

The Career Training Institute targets twelve counties, extending from the Helena area north to the Canadian border and encompassing 30,403 square miles. Because the targeted area is very rural, the Career Training Institute offers training classes in four dispersed locations: Lewistown, Great Falls, Browning, and Helena.

Montana Community Development Corporation (MCDC)
127 North Higgins
Missoula, MT 59802
E-mail: mcdc@montana.com

MCDC provides counseling, loans, and loan packaging to clients in western Montana. Professional staff have worked with hundreds of large and small businesses. MCDC has provided more than $1 million in direct business financing and has packaged and facilitated commercial loans in that amount each year.

NEVADA

The Nevada Women's Business Resource and Assistance Center (NWBRAC)
2770 S. Maryland Parkway, Suite 212
Las Vegas, NV 89109
E-mail: loftusa@aol.com

NWBRAC provides services for low- and moderate-income women in Nevada and uses the services of other providers in the state to leverage its resources. The center integrates personal development and leadership into its programs, as necessary components of business success. In a six-week prestartup course, participants assess their own skill levels and the feasibility of their ideas; determine startup costs, pricing and breakeven points; and address licensing and other startup concerns. If, at any point in the training, a client determines that entrepreneurship is not for her, she can refocus on finding employment with the center's assistance; such a decision is also seen as a success by the center. If she does decide to open a business, she takes an eight-week course that helps her develop a solid business plan. An additional course helps existing businesses address the challenges of growth, and an alumni program develops leaders and mentors from graduates and provides ongoing educational opportunities.

NEW HAMPSHIRE

Women's Business Center, Inc.
150 Greenleaf Avenue, Unit 8
Portsmouth, NH 03801
E-mail: info@womenbiz.org

The Women's Business Center (WBC) is a collaborative organization designed to encourage and support women in all phases of enterprise development. The center provides access to educational programs, financing alternatives, technical assistance, advocacy, and a network of mentors, peer advisers, and business and professional consultants. WBC addresses the needs of women business owners through seminars for women entrepreneurs, a WBC newsletter, monthly peer advisory meetings, "Internet for Small Business" workshops, and "The Entrepreneur's Advisory Network" group.

NEW JERSEY

HRD Consultants, Inc.
60 Walnut Avenue, Suite 100
Clark, NJ 07066
E-mail: hrd@aol.com
Web site: www.hrdconsultanmts.com

NEW MEXICO

Women's Economic Self-Sufficiency Team (WESST Corp.)
414 Silver SW
Albuquerque, NM 87102
E-mail: wesst@swcp.com
Web site: www.wesst.org

WESST was incorporated in 1988 to assist low-income and minority women in New Mexico. WESST Corp. clients typically need long-term training and technical assistance. The centers serve both startup and expanding businesses and provide training and counseling in both English and Spanish. Counseling and mentoring are offered through volunteer attorneys, accountants, insurance agents, and benefits counselors. Because it serves rural areas, WESST trainers often travel to clients' businesses. WESST has the only SBA MicroLoan Program

in New Mexico and is an SBA Loan Prequalification Program intermediary.

Under its newest grant, WESST serves Roswell and the surrounding seven-county area. With the closing of the Levi Strauss plant in
the fall of 1997, the area's unemployment rate jumped to more than
12 percent, with approximately one-fourth of the residents living below the poverty line.

NEW YORK

Academy for Educational Development
100 Fifth Avenue
New York, NY 10011
E-mail: earcher@aed.org
Web site: www.aed.org

International House
Women's International Leadership Center
500 Riverside Drive
New York, NY 10027
E-mail: mkim@ihouse-nyc.org
Web site: www.ihouse-nyc.org

Neighborhood Youth and Family Services
601 E. Tremont Avenue
Bronx, NY 10457
E-mail: myshamba@aol.com

Women's Venture Fund, Inc.
45 John Street, Room 1009
New York, NY 10038
E-mail: womventure@aol.com

The Women's Venture Fund, Inc., is based on a radically simple idea:
empower women, particularly low-income women, to create new
businesses by making microloans available to them, and then ensure
their success through mentoring and training. The Women's Venture
Fund makes microloans to entrepreneurial women who cannot get
funding through conventional sources. These women desperately
need small loans, business planning, and the moral support it takes
to develop a business. By addressing their credit and training needs,
the Women's Venture Fund enhances the ability of women to grow
their businesses over time.

Rockefeller Foundation
420 Fifth Avenue
New York, NY 10018–2702

NORTH CAROLINA

The North Carolina Center for Women Business Owners
230 Hay Street
Fayetteville, NC 28301
E-mail: WCOF2@aol.com
Web site: www.wcof.org

The center's mission is to be a first-step resource and referral agency for women. It has a variety of empowerment programs for women; high local credibility, with an eight-year history serving women and families; and strong local partnerships. It runs a successful entrepreneurial enterprise that provides ongoing training in product development, pricing, and marketing and gives support through its retail outlet for home-based women's businesses. Nearly one-third of clients are socially and economically disadvantaged and are from both inner city and rural areas; other clients are military spouses from two nearby bases.

NORTH DAKOTA

Women and Technology Program
1833 East Bismarck Expressway
Bismarck, ND 58504
E-mail: holt@gcentral.com

Through partnership with SBA resources, colleges and universities, and other service providers, the Women and Technology Program provides a support structure for business development and technical assistance, financial advice, business education, and market planning, primarily via distance learning. Efforts target Native Americans and welfare-to-work participants and address areas such as home-based businesses, international trade, franchising, and legal issues. Distance learning, videoconferencing, workshops, and seminars are available via Business Initiative Corporations (BIC) and tribal BICs. The program uses local resources to provide training in tiers over three years; thirteen organizations will participate in the first tier. The program reaches women in rural areas and on Indian reservations, as well as women with disabilities.

Women's Business Institute (WBI)
320 North Fifth Street, Suite 203
Fargo, ND 58107–2043
E-mail:wbinstitute@corpcomm.net
Web site: www.rrtrade.org/women/wbi

The mission of the WBI is to improve the opportunities for economic and business growth for women in North Dakota, Minnesota and the surrounding region. It offers numerous programs and services to women interested in advancing their business and career skills: monthly training classes, activities such as "Women Mean Business" networking events, coaching and counseling (including mentoring teams), and marketing/purchasing opportunities. The WBI also hosts annual events such as the Business Technology Expo, a full-day training conference, and a home-based business conference and trade show. Regular activities include computer classes, and courses in management, marketing, financing, and entrepreneurial confidence.

OHIO

Catherine S. Eberly Center for Women
Tucker Hall 0168
Toledo, Ohio 42606

Ohio Women's Business Resource Network (OWBRN)
77 South High Street, 28th Floor
Columbus, OH 43215–6108
E-mail: owbrn@eurekanet.com

The OWBRN is a statewide effort to assist women business owners and promote successful women's business ownership. An umbrella organization, it promotes the sharing of information, technical assistance, and education among its member organizations.

OREGON

ONABEN—A Native American Business Network
11825 SW Greenburg Road, Suite B3
Tigard, Oregon 97223

E-mail: kelso@onaben.org
Web site: www.onaben.org

ONABEN is a nonprofit public-benefit corporation created by northwestern Indian tribes to increase the number and profitability of
private enterprises owned by Native Americans. ONABEN offers
training, individual counseling, assisted access to markets, and facilitated access to capital on ten reservations in Oregon, Washington,
California, and Idaho. Its services are open to all citizens regardless
of tribal affiliation or ethnic background.

Southern Oregon Women's Access to Credit (SOWAC)
33 North Central, Suite 209
Medford, OR 97501
E-mail: mokief@sowac.org

Founded in 1990, SOWAC provides business training, mentoring,
and financing services to women and men who face economic hard-
ship. In 1996 and 1997 SOWAC piloted its services among low-
income Hispanic entrepreneurs and very rural entrepreneurs. In 1998
it began serving Temporary Assistance for Needy Families (TANF)
clients. In 1999, SOWAC piloted a marketing roundtable program
for its graduates who are interested in growing their businesses.
Training graduates may apply to SOWAC's Mentor Program to receive assistance from an experienced person, who volunteers expertise
over a six-month period, and for a SOWAC business loan of up to
$25,000.

PENNSYLVANIA

Allegheny West Civic Council, Inc., Women's Enterprise Center (WEC)
901 Western Avenue
Pittsburgh, PA 15233
E-mail: chloe@wecpit.org

WEC serves the Pittsburgh area and plans to establish a second location in rural Washington County. The center expects 30 percent
of its customers to be minority and about 40 percent will fall below
the federal poverty guidelines. WEC is a rural incubator offering
home-based memberships. The services they provide include a "Pass-
port for Services," a personalized written tool that sets goals and

objectives, registers customers for specific services and resources, and articulates measurable and quantifiable outcomes. Peer-to-peer forums provide an opportunity for sharing experiences. Small business development centers will subcontract for some of the technical assistance. Links to other resources, including SBA loan programs, will also be provided. The center will explore cooperative marketing among woman-owned businesses engaged in related industries on the Internet.

Women's Business Development Center (WBDC)
1315 Walnut Street, Suite 1116
Philadelphia, PA 19107–4711
E-mail: wbdc@erols.com

The Women's Business Development Center fosters business development and business retention. The center enables women to launch new businesses and to more successfully run their existing businesses. WBDC offers startup, emerging, and established entrepreneurs comprehensive support services, including "Premier FastTrac," an eleven-week program culminating in a viable business plan for each entrepreneur; the WNET program; Internet training and counseling; individualized business consulting in management, marketing, and financial matters; loan packaging; and procurement and certification assistance. By offering a full range of services and using the expertise of successful women business owners to deliver its programs, the WBDC has become a focal point for women's economic empowerment opportunities in Greater Philadelphia.

PUERTO RICO

Center for Women's Entrepreneurial Development (CWED)
San Juan and Rosales Streets
San Juan, PR 00914–0383
E-mail: carms@caribe.net

The Women's Business Institute (WBI) at University of the Sacred Heart, Center for Women's Entrepreneurial Development (CWED) offers technical assistance to women interested in establishing a business. It also provides women business owners a place to expose and share ideas, objectives, and experiences. The WBI contributes to the social and economic development of women through training on empowerment and business ownership as an alternative to attain economic independence.

RHODE ISLAND

Center for Women and Enterprise, Inc. (CWE Rhode Island)
380 Westminster Street, Suite 511
Providence, RI 02903
E-mail: cmalysz@cweprovidence.org

CWE Rhode Island is a new venture of CWE Boston, 70 percent of whose clients are women of low and very low incomes and 35 percent of whom are women of color; the new center will serve a similar population. CWE RI helps women access financing through banks and SBA loan-guarantee programs. Entrepreneurial courses include workshops, seminars, networking groups, and one-on-one counseling. CWE RI is a clearinghouse for financing, providing technical assistance on SBA loan programs and directing women business owners to local SBA partners. CWE RI offers "Turbo Day" once a year, a day-long program of high-impact workshops, each geared to a specific level of business experience. Workshops include "Shoestring Marketing," "Power Negotiating," "Super Sales Strategies," "Show Me the Money," and "Personnel: Everything You Wanted to Know but Were Afraid to Ask."

SOUTH CAROLINA

Center for Women Entrepreneurs
1301 Columbia College Drive
Columbia, SC 29203
E-mail:susdavis@colacoll.edu
Web site: www.businessforwomen.org

The mission of the Center for Women Entrepreneurs at Columbia College of South Carolina is to expand economic opportunities for women by advancing entrepreneurship and providing resources to assist in successful business startups, maintenance of growth, and exploration of new business opportunities. Services include individual consultations, management and technical assistance, an annual women's conference, a roundtable luncheon series, resource guides, seminars and workshops, and internships. The focus on communications through the Online Women's Business Center enables the project to serve not only mature women ready to start businesses or women already in business, but also entrepreneurial high school girls. As local support for this project can attest, the Center for Women Entrepreneurs is an active advocate of collaborative ventures among resources that support women entrepreneurs.

SOUTH DAKOTA

The Entrepreneur Network for Women (ENW)
100 South Maple
Watertown, SD 57201–0081
E-mail: network4women@basec.net
Web site: www.network4women.com

ENW is a statewide program offering toll-free telephone counseling, training seminars in management, marketing, financing, government contracting and entrepreneurial confidence. Networking sessions, group mentoring, and "Business Success" teams are offered at many locations in the state. ENW publishes a quarterly newsletter and holds an annual spring conference. It is a division of the Watertown Area Career Learning Center, which has assisted single parents, displaced homemakers, dislocated workers, and economically disadvantaged persons since the late 1980s. ENW collaborates with the Women's Business Institute in North Dakota.

TEXAS

Texas Center for Women's Business Enterprise (TxCWBE Austin)
4100 Ed Blustein Drive
Austin, TX 78721
E-mail: txcwbe@txcwbe.org
Web site: www.txcwbe.org

TxCWBE is a public/private initiative dedicated to the entrepreneurial success of women in Texas. TxCWBE Austin has served Texas women for more than six years. It received a new grant in 1999 to expand to the underserved Temple/Killeen area, where the population is 55 percent Anglo, 21 percent African American, and 13 percent Hispanic.

TxCWBE prepares women for business success with services and programs such as "How to Write Your Business Plan," "Fast Track to Certification," "10-Part Computer Skills Training Course," "Welfare-to-Work Hiring for Business Owners," "Conflict Resolution for Small Business Owners," and "Electronic Commerce." TxCWBE also provides services to Gatesville Correctional Facility, the largest women's prison in Texas. TxCWBE hosts a branch of the Women's Construction Network (TxCWBE originated and began hosting the network in 1993). TxCWBE holds monthly meetings to address construction-specific educational topics and procurement opportunities. TxCWBE is replicating the Women's Construction Network in the Killeen/Temple area and is broadening it to include women in agribusiness.

North Texas Women's Business Development Center, Inc. (NTWBDC)
1420 W. Mockingbird Lane
Suite 270
Dallas, TX 75247–2111
E-mail: kathy@vwbc.org
Web site: www.onlinewbc.org

Fort Worth Women's Business Center (FW WBC)
100 E. 15th Street, Suite 400
Fort Worth, TX 76102
E-mail: csimpson@fwbac.com

The FW WBC is located in the Business Assistance Center, which is a consortium of thirteen service providers established in February 1995 to serve startup and established small businesses in the Dallas/ Fort Worth area. The FW WBC will address the needs of women business owners and potential women entrepreneurs through roundtables, discussion groups, mentoring programs, networking opportunities, and training support. By leveraging local community resources, the center has helped create more than 3,350 jobs and has facilitated more than $133 million in business loans from local banks, SBA loan programs, and other community-based loan programs.

Women's Empowerment Business Center (WEBC)
2412 S. Closner
Edinburg, TX 78539
E-mail: webc@panam.edu

The WEBC serves a largely poor and Hispanic immigrant population in four counties where the unemployment rate is 20 percent and where one-third of the adult population does not have a high school education. Services are available in both English and Spanish. The WEBC is located at the SBA's one-stop capital shop in Edinburg, Texas, and works closely with other agencies and service organizations. Clients in the Enterprise Zone have access to revolving loan funds. WEBC services are integrated with those of various banks, municipalities, enterprise centers, microlenders, and chambers of commerce.

UTAH

Women's Business Center at the Chamber
175 East 400 South, Suite 600
Salt Lake City, UT 84111
E-mail: nmitchell@slacc.org
Web site: www.saltlakechamber.org

The Women's Business Center at the Chamber supports the success of women business owners in Utah with counseling, training, and loan-packaging assistance. With more than thirty committees and task forces, the chamber provides networking opportunities for clients as well as a full-service export-assistance program. The on-site high-tech center offers access to the Internet and most types of business software. Women business owners can access help with marketing, management, finance, and procurement. There is a modest fee for some services, but scholarships and specialized training are available for socially or economically disadvantaged women.

VERMONT

Commission on Women
126 State Street
Montpelier, VT 05633–6801
E-mail: info@women.state.vt.us
Web site: www.women.state.vt.us

Women's Small Business Program/Vermont Women's Business Center
208 Colchester Avenue
Burlington, VT 05401
E-mail: pgreene@charity.trinityvt.edu

The Vermont WBC focuses on economically disadvantaged women, including welfare recipients, and ensures access for people with special needs or disabilities, those in rural areas, and women interested in agriculture. Training ranges from basic to advanced, and services include financial and loan assistance, loan packaging, management and marketing assistance, and individual business counseling. Women's Network for Entrepreneurial Training (WNET) mentoring roundtables meet once a month. The center conducts a six-hour seminar on wholesale trade shows in two locations and holds an annual business showcase and conference. A subcontract with CyberSkills Vermont provides Internet training and assistance. Programs are also offered on Vermont's Interactive Television Network.

VIRGIN ISLANDS

St. Croix Foundation for Community Development, Inc. (SCFCD)
Suite 202, Chandler's Wharf
Gallows Bay
St. Croix, U.S. Virgin Islands 00820
E-mail: stxfound@worldnet.att.net

Nearly one in four Virgin Islanders does not speak English as a primary language. About one in three Virgin Islanders lives in poverty, and single women account for 50 percent of the heads of households. The SCFCD helps these women change their lives through entrepreneurship. In its first year of funding, the SCFCD is running two repeated training programs for six months each. They cover how to write a business plan, loan strategies—accessing capital for startups and expansions—and basic accounting, record keeping, small business management and marketing, and computer and Internet training. Group counseling sessions relating to the course of study are held twice a month. Mentoring and networking groups are also available. Two-hour seminars cover topics such as discipline, attitude, arts and crafts for profit, government procurement, and global marketing. Four full-day conferences are held each year.

WASHINGTON

Community Capital Development
1437 South Jackson Street, Suite 302

Seattle, WA 98122–0283
E-mail: ruthannh@seattleccd.com

The Community Capital Development program offers assistance to
the seasoned entrepreneur (in business three to five years), the business owner (in business three years or less), and the startup (including
refugee and immigrant women on welfare, and welfare-to-work participants). The center has strong local partnerships, its own in-house
loan fund, and substantial funding from the city of Seattle.

WEST VIRGINIA

Center for Economic Options, Inc.
West Virginia Microbusiness Center
214 Capitol Street, Suite 200
Charleston, WV 25301
E-mail: econoptns@citynet.net
Web site: www.centerforeconoptions.org

The Center for Economic Options is a statewide, nonprofit,
community-based organization that promotes opportunities to develop the economic capacity of West Virginia's rural communities
and their citizens, particularly women. The center creates alternative
approaches to economic development, such as networks of home-
based business entrepreneurs, and works with communities to help
build support for small and micro businesses.

WISCONSIN

Western Dairyland's Women's Business Center (WDWBC)
23122 Whitehall Road
Independence, WI 54747
E-mail: nadinej@charter.net

WDWBC serves four counties in western Wisconsin. The city of Eau
Claire, the largest population center in the service area, has the lowest
per capita personal income of any metropolitan area in the state, while
the predominantly rural nature of the service area hampers business
and economic development. WDWBC projects that at least 75 percent of its clients have incomes at or below 150 percent of the poverty
level. WDWBC provides startup assistance, access to a loan guarantee

fund, intensive follow-along services to regularly monitor progress, and continued access to a lending library of computers and related equipment. Owners of existing businesses receive customized technical assistance, for example, business-plan development, accessing financing from local lenders, SBA Loan Prequalification and MicroLoan programs, marketing assistance, and Internet training. Two types of business are especially targeted: child-care and home-based businesses. The center also shares information on Western Dairyland's sewing and textile manufacturing network, a model for flexible manufacturing that allows several micro businesses to obtain contracts and produce products that no one of the businesses could handle on its own.

Wisconsin Women's Business Initiative Corporation (WWBIC)
2745 N. Dr. Martin Luther King Jr. Drive
Milwaukee, WI 53212
E-mail: info@wwbic.com
Web site: www.wwbic.com

WWBIC has served more than 10,000 individuals and funded more than 120 business startups and more than 150 business expansions since it began in 1989 as a women's demonstration site. More than 800 jobs have been created and retained by WWBIC's efforts. WWBIC is an economic development corporation providing business education, training, and technical assistance. Its programs include peer lending, business laboratory, business incubation programs, and individual development account initiatives. WWBIC is also the state's largest microlender under SBA's MicroLoan Program. WWBIC has expanded its operations to Madison and provides training in the Milwaukee, Madison, Janesville, Fox Valley, Green Bay, Racine, and Kenosha areas.

Appendix II: Sample Business Plan

OVERVIEW

A business plan is essentially a roadmap to a desired destination. It provides a focused, targeted reference tool, which can then be used to evaluate decisions about a business. Most plans should project at least three to five years into the future. The plan itself should be limited to 15 to 30 pages, with a minimum of 10 pages. If a business plan is being used to obtain financing, it should include as many credible sources as possible. Using statistics and numbers from reliable sources will also add credibility to the plan. Avoid superlatives and purely subjective comments, which actually make the reader skeptical and reduce credibility. Where possible, use graphs, charts, and illustrations. They are visually appealing and can often communicate more clearly than words.

SAMPLE OUTLINE

I.   Executive Summary
     The Executive Summary is the most important part of the business plan and should be the last section written. The Executive Summary is where all the thoughts and plans are brought together and communicates the high points to the reader. It should be one or two pages in length.

II.   Company Description
Before presenting the detailed and more complicated aspects of the business plan, the reader needs to communicate a basic understanding of the business.

A. Company's Mission
A mission statement should provide the guiding principles behind the business. It makes a statement about what the company exists for and should be used as a focal point for writing the plan.

B. Company's Products or Services
Provide a description of each of the company's products and services. This section explains what you do.

C. Company History
This section is particularly important for an established business that is seeking financing or for buying a company. Lenders will need to have a historical perspective on the business; a later point in the plan should also give detailed financial information.

III. The Target Market
Many startups forget the simple fact that in order to have a business, you have to have customers. Every company exists to service a particular segment of the market. The plan needs to explain who those customers are in great detail.

A. Demographics
Any details that describe the potential customer are relevant. If it's a consumer, profile the typical customer with as much personal data as possible. If customers are other businesses, describe the characteristics of the average customer.

B. Geographic Issues
It is important to define the geographic area that the business will serve. It will define the marketing and sales strategy and will help to maintain focus.

C. Purchasing Patterns
Give details on how customers will buy the products or services. How often do they buy, how long between purchases, what is required for them to continue to buy?

D. Size and Trends of the Market
Given the information on the target market, now analyze what is happening to that market. Is it growing, and at what rate? What relevant trends exist in the target market that will affect future growth?

IV. Industry Analysis
It is important to have a grasp on the larger industry when planning a

competitive strategy. Lenders in particular will want to see a solid understanding of where the business fits in the overall industry.

A. Size and Growth Trends

Trade associations can be useful sources of information for industry information. Put numbers in context by comparing them to the growth in the economy as a whole. Also note seasonal aspects to growth trends.

B. Maturity of Industry

Is this a new and expanding industry, a stable industry, or an industry that is in decline? Companies at each stage of maturity face inherent risks. It is important to identify those risks so that they can be accounted for in the marketing strategy.

C. Technological Factors

It is more important than ever to look ahead to the possibility of technology replacing people in business. How can the business be improved by harnessing the multiplying factor of technology?

D. Regulatory Factors

Certain industries are particularly affected by the actions of the government. This section is meant to overview the regulations, licensing, and certification that are required for the business.

E. Vulnerability to Economic Factors

It is important to think through the company's vulnerability to swings in economic factors. How do economic shifts affect the business, and what can be done to avoid disaster when a downturn in the economy happens?

V. The Competition

Every business has competition, and if a potential new business has no competition, there probably is not much of a market for the product. Understanding the competition, and more important how to complete against them, is critical in achieving success.

A. Competitive Comparison

Compare every aspect of the product or service to those of the competition. Look at such things as price, features, quality, durability, location, and loyalty and rate the products and services in comparison with the competition's.

B. Market Share Distribution

It is important to understand who dominates the market so that the strategy is planned around them. Is the goal to take market share away from the largest competitor or fill a void left by that company's products and services? Calculate a realistic amount of market share you plan to gain; how much potential revenue does that translate into?

C. Future Competition

It is necessary to predict the future of competition. The best way to analyze this is to evaluate the barriers to entry for a new competitor. Are there high startup costs, or a particular technical expertise that would make it harder for them to enter the market? Keep in mind that in today's technological business environment, there are fewer barriers to entry. If there is profit to be made, competitors will continue to enter the market.

VI. Marketing and Sales

Marketing is a strategic activity, which is designed to create opportunities. Sales activities are tactical and are designed to create revenue. Many professionals who evaluate business plans will read this section first, since a good marketing plan is the key to growing a business.

A. Unique Positioning Statement

What is it about the products or services that are unique or compelling? How is the company's product positioned in the marketplace—as the low-cost solution or the high-value, high-cost one? What are the benefits that the customer will experience by purchasing this product or service?

B. Marketing Vehicles

How will the company market the products or services? Marketing includes communication vehicles such as advertising, direct mail, public relations, and brochures.

C. Strategic Partnerships

Strategic partnerships are a way to leverage distribution. An organization can enable other companies to sell their products by licensing agreements, franchises, or distributorships. Two companies can also agree to bundle their products.

D. Sales Plan and Forecast

It is critical to outline the sales process that will take place from initial contact to an actual sale. What are the steps that need to happen? What type of support will be needed during the process? How long, on average, will it take to complete the process? Given the attributes of the process, what is the sales forecast for the coming year?

VII. Operations

This section of the plan will be shorter than a detailed operations manual, which should also be developed for the business. Items that are of relevance in this section are items that provide a competitive edge or are unique to the way the business is run.

A. Equipment and Technology

How is technology used to improve the delivery of the product or service, or in the manufacturing process? If the business is in a technologically advanced area, this section should be more detailed.

B. Labor Requirements
What type of staff will be necessary for the business initially, and how quickly will people need to be added as the business grows?

C. Inventory Management
Inventory management even in a small business is critical for controlling costs. How will inventory be tracked and managed? What method of tracking inventory will be used?

D. Supply and Distribution
Who are the critical suppliers to the business and what alternatives are available? How is the product or service actually distributed to the customer? Does it involve a wholesaler or distributor? What are the support issues in distribution and follow-up service?

E. Research and Development
It is essential that every business have a method to continually improve the way business is done. Surveying customers is a good method for evaluating current practices. Continuing education is another way to stay current on industry trends.

VIII. Management and Operations

A. Principals and Key Employees
Good people are critical to the success of every business, particularly businesses that sell "intellectual capital." Who are the key principals of the business? What type of management or technical expertise will be required? Who are the key employees that enable the business to manufacture or sell its product or service?

B. Board of Advisers/Directors
Whether it is a formal board of directors or an informal board of advisers, every business needs a mechanism for getting feedback and advice. It is easy to lose perspective when starting or growing a business, so a plan for getting "outsider input" is critical.

C. Specialists Required
Who will the business need to draw upon for expertise in specific areas? This may include special financial or management advice, or scientific expertise. Local universities can be a resource for this type of assistance.

IX. Financials

A. Income statement

B. Cash flow

C. Balance sheet

Further Reading

Baker, Judy. *Evaluating the Impact of Development Projects on Poverty: A Handbook for Practitioners* (Washington, D.C.: World Bank, 2000).

Beyond Borders: Canadian Businesswomen in International Trade (Toronto, Ont.: Canadian Department of Foreign Affairs and International Trade, 1999).

Brush, Candida. "The Irresistible Rise of Female Entrepreneurs," *Innovation and Employment:* OECD 14 (December 1993).

Caslione, John A.; Thomas, Andrew R. *Growing Your Business in Emerging Markets: Promise and Perils* (Westport, Conn.: Quorum Books, 2000).

"Chiapas en Duda," *La Fornada* (Mexico City), May 21, 1999.

"Fast-Growth Women and Men Entrepreneurs Take Different Paths Toward Business Success" (Washington D.C.: National Foundation of Women Business Owners, 2001). Sponsored by the Edward Lowe Foundation, the Kauffman Center for Entrepreneurial Leadership and Fleet Boston Financial.

Hisrich, Robert D; Brush, Candida. *Women vs. Men Entrepreneurs: A Comparative Study* (Washington, D.C.: RISE Business, 1999).

Hudson, Brenda L. "Women's Entrepreneurship in Scotland," *Advancing Women Network*, Advancing Women.com.

Kabeer, Nalia. *Reversed Realities: Gender Hierarchies in Development Thought* (London: Verso, 1994).

Karl, Marilee. *Women and Empowerment: Participation and Decision-Making* (London: Zed Books, 1995).

Moser, Carolyn. *Gender Planning and Development: Theory, Practice, and Training* (New York: Routledge, 1993).

The New Generation of Women Business Owners: An Executive Report (Washington, D.C.: Center for Women's Business Research, 2001), underwritten by First Union Corporation.

Pauykert, Liba. "Economic Transition and Women's Employment," Paper for Employment Department, International Labor Office, Geneva, 1995.

Psacharopoulos, George. *Case Studies on Women's Employment and Pay in Latin America* (Washington, D.C.: World Bank, 1992).

"The Rise of Women Entrepreneurs," from the United Nations Development web site, www.undep.org.

Sacirby, Omar. "German Women Create Their Jobs by Starting Their Own Businesses," *Christian Science Monitor*, March 13, 1998.

"Shaking the Venture Capital Tree," *New York Times*, March 11, 2001.

Starcher, Diane. "Women Entrepreneurs: Catalysts for Transformation," *UNDEP Quarterly*, Fall 1999.

Tam, Tony. "Reducing the Gender Gap: How Important Is Increasing Women's Experience," *World Development* 24, 5 (1996).

U.S. Small Business Administration Annual Statistical Report, 1999.

U.S. Small Business Administration's Women's Online Center, www.sba.gov.

"Women at the Forefront," *Philippines Star*, April 29, 2000.

"Women Business Owners Make Profess in Access to Capital" (Washington D.C., National Foundation for Women Business Owners, 1996).

"Women Entrepreneurs in the Equity Capital Markets: The New Frontier," Washington D.C. (National Foundation of Women Business Owners, 2000). Underwritten by Wells Fargo Bank.

Woodruff, David. "A Women's Place Is in Her Own Business," *Business Week*, March 18, 1996.

"The World's Women 2000: Trends and Statistics," United Nations Department of Social Affairs, 2000.

Young, Kate. *Planning Development with Women: Making a World of Difference* (London: Macmillan, 1993).

Index

Italic type indicates a page reference to a table.